marie claire

crisp

Thunder Bay Press
An imprint of the Advantage Publishers Group
5880 Oberlin Drive, San Diego, CA 92121-4794
www.thunderbaybooks.com

All notations of errors or omissions should be addressed to Thunder Bay Press, Editorial Department, at the above address. All other correspondence (author inquiries, permissions) concerning the content of this book should be addressed to Murdoch Books Pty Limited, Pier 8/9 23 Hickson Road, Millers Point NSW 2000 Australia.

Author and Stylist: Michele Cranston
Design manager: Vivien Valk
Food preparation: Ross Dobson and Jo Glynn
Production: Monika Paratore
Photographer: Petrina Tinslay
Designer: Lauren Camilleri
Editor: Gordana Trifunovic

ISBN-13: 978-1-59223-660-2
ISBN-10: 1-59223-660-X
Library of Congress Cataloging-in-Publication Data available upon request.

Printed by 1010 Printing. Printed in China.
1 2 3 4 5 10 09 08 07 06

IMPORTANT: Those who might be at risk from the effects of salmonella poisoning (the elderly, pregnant women, young children, and those suffering from immune deficiency diseases) should consult their doctor with any concerns about eating raw eggs.

CONVERSION GUIDE: You may find cooking times vary depending on the oven you are using. For convection ovens, as a general rule, set the oven temperature to 70°F lower than indicated in the recipe. We have used 4 teaspoon to 1 tablespoon measurements. If you are using a 3 teaspoon to 1 tablespoon measure, for most recipes the difference will not be noticeable. However, for recipes using baking powder, gelatin, baking soda, or small amounts of flour and cornstarch, add an extra teaspoon for each tablespoon specified.

marie claire

crisp

michele cranston
photography by petrina tinslay

THUNDER BAY
P·R·E·S·S
San Diego, California

contents

crisp introduction

Welcome to *marie claire crisp,* a selection of our favorite recipes that are crisp and cool, fresh and summery, with handfuls of herbs and leafy greens. This is a thick and hearty book with lots of yummy ideas, which we hope will inspire you, with everything from leafy salads of crunch and color to wintry vegetables tossed in seasoned oil, warming soups, and syrupy baked apples.

I've had a lot of fun revisiting old favorites, and I hope that you have as much fun cooking and eating from our selection.

michele cranston

ingredient note

lettuce

For me, salads are all about flavor and crunch. I can think of nothing better than sitting down to a bowl of some of my favorite ingredients tossed together with a lush array of leaves and the smooth bite of a good dressing. Nowadays, with the supermarket aisles brimming with healthy bundles of leafy greens, there really is no excuse not to enjoy such simple delights.

To enjoy these delicate leaves at their best, there are a few simple rules to follow. Always buy lettuce that is in top condition. Avoid lettuce with spotted or mushy leaves and leaves that have begun to wilt. If possible, rinse the greens in cold water when you get home. Drain well and place them into plastic crisper boxes or plastic bags in the refrigerator. Prepicked leaves like arugula, spinach, mizuna, or mixed salad selections should be bought as close as possible to the day of use. Toss with a few select flavors such as eggs, cheese, canned tuna, olives, seasonal vegetables, cooked beans and lentils, charbroiled eggplant, marinated artichokes, roasted peppers, crisp apples, or finely sliced pears. The list of ingredients and possibilities are endless, so just sit back and enjoy a healthy bowlful.

ingredient note

cucumber

Crisp and green with a watery crunch, cucumbers are a bite of summer. Indeed, it's hard to imagine any summer salad without them. Think of the simplest of salads featuring lettuce, tomatoes, and cucumbers, through to Asian salads with soft strips of cucumber balancing the bite of chilis. Cucumbers are always perfect for introducing a cooling balance to hot dishes or salads with a little heat, or for providing a touch of lightness in a rich dish. Cut into chunks or julienned, they can be tossed through salads or pureed into the perfect soup for a hot midsummer evening. If you want elegant ribbons, then use a vegetable peeler to remove paper-thin strips. Toss with finely chopped herbs and use as a base to a spicy fish dish. Finely chop and toss with yogurt and mint for a smooth accompaniment to curries, or mix with a blend of herbs and avocado or tomato for a light summer salsa. There really are so many ways that they can be used to bring a lightness to summer recipes. If you wish to give the cucumbers a bit of body, then remove the liquid content by cutting them to the required size, placing into a colander, and sprinkling with salt. Allow the cucumber to sit for an hour, then squeeze out the excess liquid. Fold through a little crème fraîche and serve with smoked fish.

ingredient note

herbs

Herbs bring with them a whole world of flavors. Sage, rosemary, and oregano need to be used with a light touch. Tarragon, with its soft aniseed flavor, is wonderful sprinkled over a green salad or used to flavor sauces and dressings. Dill is marvelous with fish and potatoes, while chives can be sprinkled over anything that's leafy, eggy, or fishy. Some herbs bring a lightness and freshness to certain recipes, and these I tend to use by the handful. Lush and leafy parsley is welcome in almost any salad or richly flavored meal. It's not too strong to overpower other flavors but still has enough freshness to lift the spirits of just about anything. Arugula has become a salad standard and can usually be bought as bunches of large leaves or as loose small leaves. Some varieties are particularly peppery and so should be mixed with other leaves or with strong flavors that will balance its bite. And cilantro, with its particular flavor, is ideally suited to the vibrant ingredients found in Asian or Middle Eastern cuisines.

Whether cooked or eaten fresh, enjoy herbs for the smile that they'll bring to your mouth.

ingredient note

green apples

Crunchy and green, juicy and sweet with just enough sour, green apples may make a delicious mouthful, but they also make a fantastic base for many classic dishes. While apples are wonderful freshly sliced into a summery salad, they really come into their own when cooked. It's no wonder that apple pie and Mom has become such a cliché, since any dessert involving baked apples is instantly nostalgic and comforting. I have fond childhood memories of steamy bowls of stewed apples served with custard, along with the distinct memories of fighting with my siblings for the curly green tails of skin that were peeled from the apples. Those slivers of green were a crunchy foretaste of good things to come.

Apples can be sliced over the top of a cake batter and sprinkled with cinnamon sugar, or baked with other fruits into a wintry crumble. They can be lightly stewed with a little orange juice and butter, or baked into a fluffy explosion of syrupy juices. Finely sliced, they can be fanned over puff pastry for a delicately perfect taste of apple, or richly caramelized to form the base of the justly famous tarte tatin. Add some dollops of cream, vanilla ice cream, caramel ice cream, or custard, and who could stop at just one helping?

green papaya salad rice paper rolls fried green olives seared tuna with lime leaf and peanuts thai fish cakes salmon and chive fritters smoked trout and pickled cucumber on oatcakes pickled swordfish zucchini and marjoram frittatas lemon curry scallops cheese and olive sandwiches caper and polenta muffins with smoked salmon crab cocktail in a leaf salad of avocado and preserved lemon scallop and

01 starters and sides

cilantro wontons crab with lemon, parsley, and chili lime and coconut pancakes with chicken and mint sage and polenta madeleines scallops with ginger and lemongrass caesar salad buttered roast asparagus cucumber tea sandwiches oysters with lime green

steamed mussels with thai salsa

serves 4

4 1/2 pounds mussels in the shell
2 cups white wine
2 tablespoons shaved jaggery (or brown sugar)
1 tablespoon fish sauce
2 tablespoons lime juice
1 red chili, seeded and thinly sliced
2 Lebanese (short) cucumbers, finely diced
1 tablespoon finely diced red bell pepper
15 mint leaves, thinly sliced
lime wedges, to serve

Clean the mussels in a sink filled with cold water, removing the beards and any barnacles from the shells. Discard any mussels that remain closed and don't open when you tap them. Put in a large pan and pour in the wine. Cover with a tight-fitting lid and cook over high heat, shaking the pan occasionally. Check after 4 minutes, removing any mussels that have opened. If any stay closed, return them to the heat for a minute, then discard any that still haven't opened. Allow the mussels to cool.

Put the jaggery, fish sauce, and lime juice in a bowl and stir until the jaggery has dissolved. Add the chili, cucumber, bell pepper, and mint. Mix together.

Break the top shells off the mussels so that the meat is left sitting on a half-shell. Arrange the mussels on a serving platter and spoon a little salsa into each one. Serve with lime wedges.

thai-style papaya salad

makes 20

1 small green papaya (about 9 ounces)
1 red chili, seeded and finely chopped
3 tablespoons lime juice
2 tablespoons fish sauce
3 tablespoons shaved jaggery (or brown sugar)
2 garlic cloves, crushed
2 tablespoons dried Asian fried onions
4 large handfuls mint, roughly chopped
20 butterhead lettuce leaves, washed and drained

Coarsely grate the green papaya and set aside.

Make a dressing by combining the chili, lime juice, fish sauce, jaggery, and garlic in a bowl. Stir to dissolve the jaggery.

Just before serving, combine the papaya, fried onions, mint, and dressing in a bowl. Put a tablespoon of the papaya mixture in each of the lettuce leaves and serve.

rice paper rolls

makes 12

1 handful cilantro leaves
1 cup grated green papaya
1/2 cup bean sprouts, roughly chopped
6 mint leaves, finely chopped
2 tablespoons finely diced red bell pepper
12 rice paper sheets
lime wedges, to serve

dipping sauce
1 1/2 tablespoons sugar
3 tablespoons lime juice
1 1/2 tablespoons fish sauce
1/2 garlic clove, finely chopped
1 small red chili, seeded and finely chopped

To make the dipping sauce, combine the sugar, lime juice, fish sauce, garlic, and chili in a small bowl. Stir until the sugar has dissolved. Set aside.

Put the cilantro, green papaya, bean sprouts, mint, and bell pepper in a bowl and stir to combine.

Fill a large bowl with warm water and soak one of the rice paper sheets until it is just soft. Remove to a clean work surface and place a spoonful of the papaya mixture into the lower section of the sheet. Fold the two sides over so that they slightly overlap, then roll the sheet up. You should have a neat parcel. Set aside and repeat with the remaining rice sheets.

Serve the rolls with the lime wedges and dipping sauce.

fried green olives

makes 20

2 tablespoons finely chopped Italian parsley
1/3 cup crumbled feta cheese
20 large green olives, pitted
1/4 cup all-purpose flour
1 egg, lightly beaten
1/2 cup fine dry bread crumbs
1/2 cup vegetable oil

Put the parsley and feta in a bowl and stir well. Stuff a little of the mixture into the center of each olive.

Put the flour in a shallow bowl, the egg in a small bowl, and the bread crumbs in another bowl. Heat the oil in a deep frying pan over medium heat. Toss the olives, a few at a time, in the flour, then dip into the beaten egg, and finally roll in the bread crumbs. Fry the olives in the oil for 1 minute or until golden brown. Remove from the pan and drain on paper towels. Repeat with the remaining olives.

seared tuna with lime leaf and peanuts

makes 30

- $2^1/_2$ tablespoons tamarind water (see basics)
- 1 tablespoon roughly chopped jaggery (or brown sugar)
- 4 tablespoons lime juice
- 1 tablespoon grated fresh ginger
- 1 tablespoon fish sauce
- 2 teaspoons sesame oil
- 1 red chili, seeded and finely chopped
- 1 tablespoon finely chopped Kaffir lime leaves
- 1 tablespoon finely chopped lemongrass, white part only
- vegetable oil, for cooking
- $10^1/_2$ ounces tuna fillet, cut into small pieces
- sea salt, for seasoning
- 3 thin Lebanese (short) cucumbers, peeled
- 1 large handful cilantro leaves, finely chopped
- $^1/_2$ cup peanuts, toasted and finely chopped

Put the tamarind water, jaggery, lime juice, ginger, fish sauce, sesame oil, chili, lime leaves, and lemongrass in a small bowl and stir well to dissolve the jaggery.

Lightly oil a frying pan, place over high heat, and sear the tuna for 1 minute on each side. Remove from the heat and season with a little sea salt.

Slice the cucumbers into $^1/_4$-inch rounds and top with a slice of tuna. Toss the cilantro and peanuts in the dressing. Put a teaspoon of dressing onto each of the tuna slices and serve.

thai fish cakes

makes 20

1 pound red snapper fillets
2 tablespoons fish sauce
1 tablespoon red curry paste
1 egg
1 teaspoon shaved jaggery (or brown sugar)
3 Kaffir lime leaves, thinly sliced
15 green beans
1 large red chili
sunflower oil, for cooking
sweet chili sauce, to serve

Put the fish fillets in a food processor with the fish sauce, curry paste, egg, jaggery, and lime leaves. Process until the mixture is smooth.

Slice the beans into thin rounds. Remove the seeds from the chili and finely chop. Stir the beans and chili into the pureed fish.

Roll 1 rounded tablespoon of mixture into a ball and then flatten it a little. Set aside and repeat with the remaining mixture. Heat the oil in a large frying pan over medium to high heat and fry the fish cakes, a few at a time, until golden brown on both sides. Drain on paper towels. Serve with sweet chili sauce.

pickled swordfish

makes 20

2$^1/_2$ tablespoons olive oil
2 red onions, thinly sliced
1–2 small red chilies, seeded and finely chopped
2 garlic cloves, crushed
2 ripe tomatoes, finely diced
1 teaspoon sea salt
14 ounces swordfish fillets, boned, skin removed, and finely diced
3 handfuls mint
4 lemons, juiced
20 baby mignonette or romaine lettuce leaves, washed and drained
sea salt and freshly ground black pepper, to season

Heat the olive oil in a frying pan over medium heat, add the onions, and gently cook for 5–7 minutes, stirring, until soft and transparent. Stir in the chilies, garlic, tomatoes, and sea salt. Remove from the heat and set aside to cool.

Put the raw fish pieces in a single layer in a wide ceramic or glass dish. Cover with the onion mixture and mint, and add enough lemon juice to cover all the ingredients. Cover and leave to marinate in the refrigerator for 24 hours.

To serve, put a small amount of pickled fish in the center of each lettuce leaf and season with a sprinkle of sea salt and some freshly ground black pepper.

smoked trout and pickled cucumber on oatcakes

makes 24

2 Lebanese (short) cucumbers, sliced in half lengthwise
1 teaspoon salt
2 tablespoons lemon juice
7 ounces smoked trout, flaked
1/3 cup sour cream
1 tablespoon finely chopped lemon zest
salt and freshly ground black pepper, to season
24 oatcakes (see basics)
1 tablespoon dill

Use a teaspoon to scoop out the seeds from the cucumbers. Thinly slice them, then sprinkle the flesh with salt. Put in a colander over a bowl and leave for 1 hour. Squeeze the cucumber of all liquid, then pat dry with paper towels. Place in a bowl with 2 teaspoons of the lemon juice and mix.

In another bowl, combine the trout, sour cream, and lemon zest. Season with salt and freshly ground black pepper. Add the remaining lemon juice, a little at a time, tasting as you go. Put a teaspoon of the trout mixture on the oatcakes and top with a little of the cucumber. Sprinkle with dill.

salmon and chive fritters

makes 36

9 ounces salmon fillet, boned and skin removed
1 tablespoon finely chopped lemon zest
2 eggs, lightly beaten
1 cup all-purpose flour
1 teaspoon baking powder
2 tablespoons plain yogurt
1/2 cup thinly sliced garlic chives
1 cup thinly sliced scallions
salt and freshly ground black pepper, to season
vegetable oil, for cooking
lemon wedges, to serve

Cut the salmon into 1/2-inch dice. Put in a small bowl, cover, and refrigerate until ready to use.

Put the lemon zest, eggs, flour, baking powder, and yogurt in a bowl and whisk until smooth. Just before cooking, fold the salmon, garlic chives, and scallions through the batter until evenly mixed. Season well with salt and freshly ground black pepper.

Heat a large frying pan over medium heat and add 1 tablespoon of the oil. Put rounded teaspoons of the mixture into the pan and press down to form flat fritters. As each fritter becomes golden on the bottom, turn it over and cook the other side. Remove and drain on paper towels. Repeat this process, adding a little more oil to the pan as necessary. Serve warm with the lemon wedges.

zucchini and marjoram frittatas

makes 24

1 tablespoon butter
1 red onion, thinly sliced
1 teaspoon finely chopped marjoram
1 1/2 cups grated zucchini
6 eggs
salt and white pepper, to season
1/2 cup grated fresh Parmesan cheese

Preheat the oven to 350°F. Heat the butter in a frying pan. Sauté the onion and marjoram over medium heat for 7–10 minutes or until the onion is soft and caramelized. Spoon the mixture into two lightly greased, 12-hole mini muffin pans. Top with the zucchini.

Whisk the eggs with 1 tablespoon of water and season with salt and white pepper. Fill each of the muffin holes with the egg mixture and sprinkle with the Parmesan. Bake for 10 minutes or until set.

lemon curry scallops

serves 4

1 teaspoon butter
2 shallots, finely diced
1 teaspoon green curry paste
1 tablespoon finely chopped lemongrass, white part only
2/3 cup unsweetened coconut cream
1 lemon, juiced
16 scallops in the shell, cleaned
1 handful cilantro leaves
lime wedges, to serve

Put the butter, shallots, curry paste, and lemongrass in a small saucepan over low to medium heat. Cook for 3 minutes. Add the coconut cream and simmer for 2 minutes, then stir in the lemon juice.

Put the scallops, still in their shells, under a hot broiler for 2–3 minutes.

Spoon a little of the sauce over each scallop. Sprinkle with cilantro and serve with lime wedges.

cheese and olive sandwiches

makes 12 small slices

- 1/3 cup pitted and thinly sliced green olives
- 2/3 cup grated fresh mozzarella cheese
- 1/3 cup grated fresh Parmesan cheese
- 2 tablespoons roughly chopped Italian parsley
- 8 slices white bread, crusts removed
- 2 tablespoons olive oil

Preheat the oven to 350°F. Put the olives, mozzarella, Parmesan, and parsley in a bowl and mix well.

Brush four slices of bread with half the olive oil and place them, oiled side down, on a greased baking sheet. Divide the cheese mixture evenly between the four slices of bread and top with the remaining slices. Brush the tops of the sandwiches with the remaining oil and place in the oven for 5 minutes. Flip the sandwiches over and cook for a further 5 minutes to ensure they are golden brown on both sides.

Remove and slice each sandwich into three fingers.

caper and polenta muffins with smoked salmon

makes 18

- $1\frac{1}{2}$ cups all-purpose flour
- $\frac{2}{3}$ cup polenta
- 2 teaspoons baking powder
- 2 tablespoons salted capers, rinsed and drained
- 1 large handful roughly chopped Italian parsley
- $\frac{1}{2}$ teaspoon finely chopped tarragon
- freshly ground black pepper, to season
- 1 cup milk
- 2 tablespoons olive oil
- 1 egg
- $\frac{1}{3}$ cup sour cream
- 6 ounces smoked salmon
- wasabi roe or fresh dill, to garnish

Preheat the oven to 350°F. Put the flour, polenta, baking powder, capers, parsley, and tarragon in a bowl and mix well. Season with some freshly ground black pepper. In a pitcher, whisk together the milk, oil, and egg. Pour into the bowl of dry ingredients and fold through until just combined. Spoon the mixture into a greased mini muffin pan and bake for 20 minutes.

When completely cool, cut off the tops of the muffins. Top with sour cream and a little of the smoked salmon. Garnish with wasabi roe or dill.

crab cocktail in leaves

makes 16-20

2 egg yolks
1 lemon, zested and juiced
1 cup light olive oil
1 teaspoon Dijon mustard
2 teaspoons finely chopped tarragon
1 tablespoon tomato paste
1 1/2 cups fresh cooked crabmeat
salt and pepper, to season
16–20 little gem (small romaine) lettuce leaves
Tabasco sauce, to serve

Whisk together the egg yolks and lemon zest and juice in a bowl. Slowly drizzle in the oil, whisking the mixture until it becomes thick and creamy. Fold in the mustard, tarragon, and tomato paste. Set aside.

Break up the crabmeat with a fork, leaving it in fairly large pieces, then fold it into the dressing and season well with salt and pepper. Spoon the crab into the lettuce leaves and top each with a dash of Tabasco.

salad of avocado and preserved lemon

serves 6

2 avocados
3 Lebanese (short) cucumbers
2 tablespoons finely chopped preserved lemon
4 tablespoons cilantro leaves, roughly chopped
2 tablespoons virgin olive oil
1 tablespoon lemon juice

Remove the skin and pit from the avocados. Cut into bite-size chunks. Halve the cucumbers lengthwise, then slice into thick pieces diagonally. Put the avocado, cucumber, preserved lemon, cilantro, olive oil, and lemon juice in a bowl and lightly toss together without breaking up the avocado. Serve with fish or as a side salad.

scallop and cilantro wontons

makes 30

14 ounces white scallop meat, finely diced
1/2 teaspoon grated orange zest
1/4 cup thinly sliced scallions
3 tablespoons finely chopped cilantro leaves
1/4 teaspoon sesame oil
2 teaspoons finely chopped red chilies
1 teaspoon fish sauce
1 Kaffir lime leaf, shredded
1/4 teaspoon grated fresh ginger
2 tablespoons all-purpose flour
salt and pepper, to season
1 egg
30 square wonton skins
peanut oil, for deep-frying
lime wedges, to serve

Combine the scallop meat, orange zest, scallions, cilantro, sesame oil, chilies, fish sauce, lime leaf, and ginger in a bowl. Sprinkle the flour over the top, season with salt and pepper, and stir well. Lightly beat the egg with 1/4 cup of water.

Put a wonton skin on a clean surface and place 1 rounded teaspoon of the scallop mixture into the center. Brush the egg wash along the edges. Bring the corners together, seal the sides, then twist the top firmly. Repeat with the remaining mixture.

Heat the oil in a wok and cook the wontons in batches until golden brown. Remove and drain on paper towels. Serve with lime wedges.

crab with lemon, parsley, and chili on toasts

makes 40

10 slices white bread, crusts removed
2 1/2 tablespoons olive oil
1 1/2 cups fresh cooked crabmeat, shredded
2 tablespoons grated lemon zest
1 tablespoon virgin olive oil
1 small red chili, seeded and finely chopped
2 tablespoons finely chopped Italian parsley
2 teaspoons lemon juice
40 basil leaves

Preheat the oven to 315°F. Cut each slice of bread into four circles using a cookie cutter. Place on a baking sheet, lightly brush with olive oil, and bake until golden brown. Allow to cool.

Put the crabmeat in a bowl, add the remaining ingredients except the basil leaves, and stir well to combine. Place a basil leaf onto each of the little toasts and top with a rounded teaspoon of the crab mixture. Serve immediately.

Note: The crab mixture will keep well for several hours, so it can easily be prepared in advance.

lime and coconut pancakes with chicken and mint

makes 20

2/3 cup lime juice
2 teaspoons sesame oil
2 tablespoons shaved jaggery (or brown sugar)
2 teaspoons fish sauce
1 teaspoon seeded and finely chopped red chili
14 ounces chicken, poached and shredded
1 cup all-purpose flour
1/4 teaspoon salt
1 egg, lightly beaten
1 lime, zested and juiced
1 cup unsweetened coconut milk
1 large handful mint
3 handfuls cilantro leaves

Combine the lime juice, sesame oil, jaggery, fish sauce, and chili in a bowl and stir to dissolve the jaggery. Add the chicken.

To make the pancakes, sift the flour and salt into a bowl. Make a well in the center and stir in the egg, lime zest and juice, and coconut milk. Whisk to form a smooth batter. Grease a large nonstick frying pan and place over low heat. Drizzle in the batter in a cobweb of lines, making a circle 4 inches in diameter. Leave to cook for 2 minutes, then flip over and cook for another 1–2 minutes or until golden. Transfer to a plate and repeat with the remaining pancake mixture.

Before serving, toss the mint and cilantro through the chicken. Top each pancake with some of the chicken salad. Roll up and serve.

walnut bread with creamed goat cheese and pear

makes 50

1 cup fresh goat cheese
1/2 cup whipping cream
salt and freshly ground black pepper, to season
50 pieces walnut bread (see basics)
2 ripe pears

Combine the goat cheese and cream in a bowl. Season with salt and freshly ground black pepper.

To assemble, spread a small amount of the goat cheese mixture on top of each slice of walnut bread. Cut the pears into thin wedges and place on top of the cheese.

sage and polenta madeleines

makes 24

- 2/3 cup unsalted butter, softened
- 2 teaspoons sugar
- 2 egg yolks
- 2 eggs
- 1/3 cup all-purpose flour
- 1/3 cup fine polenta
- 1 1/4 teaspoons baking powder
- 1 1/4 teaspoons salt
- 1 1/4 teaspoons coarsely ground black pepper
- 24 small sage leaves

Preheat the oven to 350°F. Put 2 tablespoons of the butter in a small saucepan and cook over high heat until the butter begins to brown. Remove from the heat and set aside.

Cream the remaining butter and the sugar in a mixing bowl until pale and fluffy. Gradually add the egg yolks and whole eggs, beating well after each addition. Slowly fold in the flour, polenta, baking powder, salt, and black pepper.

Grease a madeleine pan with the browned butter, place a sage leaf in the base of each mold, and top with a teaspoon of batter. If you don't have a madeleine pan, use a shallow muffin pan. Bake for 7–10 minutes or until golden and springy to the touch. Remove from the tray and cool on a wire rack.

scallops with ginger and lemongrass

serves 4

2 tablespoons finely chopped lemongrass, white part only
2 teaspoons grated fresh ginger
1/2 red chili, seeded and finely chopped
1 tablespoon sesame oil
2 tablespoons mirin
1 tablespoon fish sauce
1 lime, juiced
12 scallops in the shell, cleaned
cilantro leaves, to serve
lime wedges, to serve

Combine the lemongrass, ginger, chili, sesame oil, mirin, fish sauce, and lime juice in a bowl. Leave to infuse for a few minutes.

Spoon a little of the marinade over the scallops and arrange them, still in their shells, in two steamer baskets. Put the two baskets over a saucepan of simmering water. Cover and steam for 4 minutes, swapping the position of the baskets after 2 minutes. Carefully remove the scallops from the baskets without letting any of the juices escape from the shells. Sprinkle with cilantro and serve with lime wedges.

caesar salad cups

makes approximately 24

10 slices white bread, crusts removed
1 garlic clove, crushed
6 anchovies, shredded
1 egg yolk
1/2 teaspoon Worcestershire sauce
2 tablespoons lemon juice
freshly ground black pepper, to season
3/4 cup vegetable or light olive oil
1/2 cup grated fresh Parmesan cheese
3 mignonette or red leaf lettuce heads, leaves washed and drained

Preheat the oven to 300°F. Slice the bread into 1/4-inch cubes. Place on a baking sheet and toast in the oven until crisp and golden. Allow the croutons to cool.

Put the garlic, anchovies, egg yolk, Worcestershire sauce, lemon juice, and some freshly ground black pepper in a bowl and blend together. Whisk the mixture continuously while slowly pouring in the oil to form a thick mayonnaise. Fold the Parmesan and croutons into the mayonnaise.

Thinly slice any large lettuce leaves and add them to the mayonnaise. Spoon the mixture into the small lettuce leaves and serve immediately.

spinach, black bean, and orange wontons

makes 24

2 bunches spinach (about 2 pounds), washed and trimmed
1 orange, zest grated
3 tablespoons Chinese salted black beans, rinsed
1 tablespoon shaved jaggery (or brown sugar)
1 tablespoon Chinese rice wine
1/2 teaspoon sesame oil
24 square wonton skins
sweet chili sauce, to serve

Blanch the spinach until emerald green. Drain and set aside to cool. Finely chop the spinach leaves and put them in a bowl with the orange zest and black beans.

Put the jaggery, Chinese rice wine, and sesame oil in a small bowl. Stir until the jaggery has dissolved, and then pour the sauce over the spinach. Stir to combine the filling ingredients.

Put a wonton skin on a clean surface and moisten the edges with a little water. Put 1 rounded teaspoon of the mixture in the center, bring the four corners together, and pinch to seal the edges. Repeat with the remaining mixture and wonton skins.

Put the wontons into a steamer basket, place over a saucepan of boiling water, and steam for 10–12 minutes. Serve with sweet chili sauce.

buttery roasted asparagus

serves 4

3 tablespoons butter
20 thin asparagus spears, trimmed
4 slices whole-wheat bread, toasted
1 lemon, for juice
1/3 cup shaved fresh Parmesan cheese

Preheat the oven to 350°F. Put a roasting pan on the stove top over low heat and add the butter. When the butter has melted, add the asparagus. Season with salt and pepper. Roll the asparagus around to coat in the butter, and then put the asparagus in the oven and roast for 10 minutes.

Arrange the toast on four plates and top with some asparagus. Squeeze a little lemon juice into the roasting pan, swirl it around, and then drizzle the pan juices over the asparagus. Top with the Parmesan.

fennel and grapefruit salad with rich apple dressing

serves 4

2 cups apple juice
3 black peppercorns
2 thyme sprigs
1 tablespoon balsamic vinegar
1 teaspoon celery salt
2 fennel bulbs, trimmed, very thinly sliced
2 pink grapefruit, peeled, segments removed
2 celery stalks, thinly sliced
salt and freshly ground black pepper, to season

To make the apple dressing, put the apple juice, peppercorns, and thyme in a small saucepan over medium heat. Bring to a boil and reduce the liquid until it is syrupy and there is about 1/4 cup liquid left in the pan. Set aside and allow to cool. Stir in the balsamic vinegar and celery salt.

Pile the fennel, grapefruit, and celery on a serving platter and drizzle with the dressing. Season with salt and freshly ground black pepper. Serve with cold roast pork or chicken.

cucumber tea sandwiches

makes 18 small slices

2 tablespoons finely chopped dill
2½ tablespoons butter, softened
12 thin slices bread, crusts removed
2 Lebanese (short) cucumbers, thinly sliced
freshly ground black pepper, to season

Fold the dill through the softened butter and spread lightly onto the slices of bread. Place the thinly sliced cucumber on six of the bread slices. Season with freshly ground black pepper and top with the remaining bread. Cut each sandwich into three fingers. Serve immediately.

oysters with lime

makes 24

1 tablespoon lime juice
1 teaspoon black sesame seeds
1/4 teaspoon sesame oil
1 tablespoon finely diced Lebanese (short) cucumber
24 freshly shucked oysters

Combine the lime juice, sesame seeds, oil, and cucumber in a small bowl. Serve the oysters accompanied with the dressing.

whitebait fritters

makes 20

1 cup all-purpose flour
1/2 teaspoon cayenne pepper
1 teaspoon grated lemon zest
1 egg
1 tablespoon butter, melted
3 tablespoons milk
1 teaspoon salt
9 ounces small whitebait
3 tablespoons finely chopped Italian parsley
vegetable oil, for frying
lime wedges, to serve

Put the flour in a food processor. Add the cayenne pepper, lemon zest, egg, butter, milk, and salt. Process to form a thick batter. Spoon into a bowl and stir in the whitebait and parsley.

Heat some vegetable oil in a deep, heavy-based frying pan over medium heat. To test if the oil is sizzling hot, drop in a little batter—it should sizzle when it is ready. Drop small spoonfuls of the batter into the oil and fry on each side until golden brown. Remove and drain on paper towels. Serve while warm with lime wedges.

fennel rémoulade

serves 4

2 egg yolks
1 lemon, juiced
1 cup oil
1 tablespoon Dijon mustard
sea salt, to season
3 large fennel bulbs, trimmed
1 handful Italian parsley
4 slices heavy rye bread, toasted

Whisk the egg yolks and lemon juice together in a bowl. Slowly drizzle in the oil, whisking until the mixture becomes thick and creamy. Stir in the mustard and season to taste with sea salt. Set the mayonnaise aside.

Slice the fennel into paper-thin slices, then chop. Add to the mayonnaise and stir until the fennel is well coated, then add the parsley. Serve with rye toast.

mozzarella, artichoke, and parsley crostini

makes 12

6-ounce jar marinated artichoke hearts
1 tablespoon roughly chopped Italian parsley
white pepper, to season
1 baguette
olive oil, for brushing
1 cup thinly sliced fresh mozzarella cheese
parsley leaves, to garnish
extra-virgin olive oil, for drizzling

Preheat the oven to 300°F. Drain the artichoke hearts and put them in a food processor with the chopped parsley. Season with a little white pepper and process to a smooth paste.

Cut the baguette into twelve thin slices and brush one side of each slice with olive oil. Put the slices on a baking sheet and bake until golden brown, turning them once. Remove from the oven and spread the artichoke paste on top of the crostini. Top with the mozzarella, garnish with a parsley leaf, and drizzle with the olive oil.

steamed salmon with fennel and mint

makes 20

2 teaspoons mustard seeds
1/2 teaspoon fennel seeds
2 teaspoons sugar
1/4 teaspoon salt
2 tablespoons olive oil
1/2 teaspoon white vinegar
1 cup coarsely grated fennel
1 Lebanese (short) cucumber, thinly sliced
1 large handful mint, thinly sliced
4 tablespoons lemon juice
7 ounces salmon fillet, boned and skin removed
20 scallop shells or Chinese spoons, for serving

Put the mustard seeds, fennel seeds, sugar, and salt in a mortar and pestle and grind until the fennel seeds have been crushed. Add the oil and vinegar and stir to form a thick dressing.

Combine the fennel, cucumber, mint, and lemon juice in a bowl. Pour the dressing over the salad and mix well.

Slice the salmon into ten thin strips and then slice each in half again, giving you twenty 3 1/4 x 1 1/2 x 1/4–inch pieces. Place a piece of salmon on each of the shells or spoons. Put the shells in a bamboo steamer over a saucepan of boiling water. Cover and steam for 2 minutes. Remove the shells from the basket and top with the fennel salad. Serve immediately.

avocado on sourdough

serves 4

8 slices thickly cut sourdough bread
1 garlic clove, lightly crushed
4 vine-ripened tomatoes, sliced
2 avocados, cut into wedges
sea salt and freshly ground black pepper, to season
2 tablespoons extra-virgin olive oil

Lightly toast the sourdough bread on one side, then rub the garlic clove over the toasted surface. Arrange the tomato slices on the bread and top with wedges of avocado. Season liberally with sea salt and freshly ground black pepper. Drizzle with the olive oil and serve.

orange and watercress salad

serves 4

3 leeks, trimmed
2 tablespoons olive oil
1 tablespoon soy sauce
3 oranges, peeled and thinly sliced into rings
1 bunch watercress (about 14 ounces), cleaned and sorted
2 tablespoons extra-virgin olive oil
freshly ground black pepper, to season

Slice the leeks in half lengthwise, then rinse well in a large bowl of cold water. Cut the leeks into 1 1/4-inch lengths and thinly slice. Put the leeks and oil in a large saucepan over medium heat. Cover and simmer for 10 minutes or until the leeks are soft. Drizzle with the soy sauce, remove, and allow to cool. Layer the orange rings with the leeks and watercress. Drizzle with extra-virgin olive oil and season with freshly ground black pepper.

chicken and herb tea sandwiches

makes 24 triangles

10½ ounces boneless, skinless chicken thighs
1 handful Italian parsley, roughly chopped
2 teaspoons olive oil
1 teaspoon thyme
1 teaspoon salt
2 teaspoons finely chopped chives
2 teaspoons finely chopped mint
2½ tablespoons butter, softened
12 thin slices white bread, crusts removed
salt and freshly ground black pepper, to season

Preheat the oven to 350°F. Put the chicken and parsley in a small baking dish, add the oil, and sprinkle with thyme and salt. Cover with foil and bake for 30 minutes. Allow the chicken to cool, then finely chop or shred the flesh.

Fold the chives and mint through the softened butter and spread lightly onto the slices of bread. Divide the chicken equally between six slices of bread, season with salt and freshly ground black pepper, and top with the remaining slices of bread. Cut each sandwich into four triangles and serve immediately.

sashimi tuna with spinach and sesame

makes 30

7 ounces sashimi tuna
1/2 bunch spinach (9 ounces), washed and trimmed
1 teaspoon superfine sugar
2 tablespoons soy sauce
1/3 cup sesame seeds
2 teaspoons mirin

Put the tuna in the freezer for 30–35 minutes. (This firms the tuna, making it easier to slice thinly.) Plunge the spinach leaves into salted boiling water for 20 seconds, then remove and put in a bowl of iced water. Drain and squeeze out any excess water, then shred finely.

In a small bowl, dissolve the sugar in the soy sauce. Roast the sesame seeds in a frying pan over medium heat, removing the pan from the heat when the seeds begin to pop. Roughly grind or chop the seeds. Put them in a bowl along with the mirin, soy sauce mixture, and the spinach.

With a sharp knife, slice the tuna very thinly to make 30 slices. Put one of the slices onto a clean work surface. Take 1 teaspoon of the spinach mixture, squeeze it of any liquid, and put it at one end of the tuna. Roll up the tuna and place on a serving platter. Repeat with the remaining tuna and spinach. Serve immediately.

guacamole

serves 4-6

1 red chili, seeded and finely chopped
2 limes, juiced
3 tablespoons olive oil
2 scallions, thinly sliced
3 tablespoons finely chopped cilantro leaves
1 Lebanese (short) cucumber, finely diced
1 ripe tomato
2 avocados

Put the chili in a bowl. Add the lime juice, olive oil, scallions, cilantro, and cucumber. Cut the tomato in half, scoop out the seeds, and finely dice the flesh. Add the tomato flesh to the bowl and stir the ingredients together. Cut the avocados in half and remove the pits. With a small sharp knife, cut the flesh into a small dice using crisscrossing lines. Run a large spoon between the skin and the flesh, and scoop out the diced avocado. Add to the bowl and lightly fold to combine. Serve with corn chips or toasted tortilla triangles.

bean salad

serves 4

3 tablespoons extra-virgin olive oil
1 tablespoon lemon juice
1 teaspoon walnut oil
1/2 teaspoon superfine sugar
1/2 teaspoon Dijon mustard
freshly ground black pepper and sea salt, to season
4 cups green beans, trimmed
14-ounce can lima beans, drained and rinsed
1 handful Italian parsley, chopped

Put the olive oil, lemon juice, walnut oil, sugar, and mustard in a large bowl and season liberally with freshly ground black pepper and sea salt. Whisk with a fork until combined.

Blanch the green beans in boiling water until they begin to turn bright green, then quickly drain and add to the bowl. Toss the green beans until they are well coated in the dressing. Allow to cool, then add the lima beans and parsley and toss again. Serve with seared tuna or barbecued steaks.

asparagus with lemon crumbs

serves 4

2 slices whole-wheat bread
1 garlic clove
1 teaspoon sea salt
1 teaspoon thyme
1/2 teaspoon roughly chopped rosemary
1 lemon, zested and juiced
1 tablespoon olive oil
24 asparagus spears, trimmed
2 1/2 tablespoons unsalted butter, chilled and cut into cubes
1/4 cup finely grated fresh Parmesan cheese

Preheat the oven to 400°F. Remove the crusts and put the bread in a food processor with the garlic, sea salt, thyme, rosemary, lemon zest, and olive oil. Process until bread crumbs form. Sprinkle the crumbs in a shallow baking dish and bake in the oven until golden. Blanch the asparagus until it is bright green, then drain and rinse in cold water. Put the lemon juice in a small saucepan over medium heat. Whisk in the cold butter. Remove from the heat when the butter has melted.

Divide the asparagus between four small plates and sprinkle with the bread crumbs and Parmesan. Drizzle with the warm lemon sauce and serve.

nori salsa

serves 4

1 Lebanese (short) cucumber, julienned
1/2 daikon, julienned
1 tablespoon finely chopped pickled ginger
a few drops of sesame oil
1/2 teaspoon red chili powder
1 tablespoon rice vinegar
2 teaspoons sesame seeds, toasted
1 nori sheet

Put the cucumber in a bowl with the daikon, ginger, sesame oil, chili powder, rice vinegar, and sesame seeds.

Preheat the oven to 350°F. Take the nori sheet and lightly toast in the oven until crisp. Using a pair of kitchen scissors, cut the toasted nori sheet into thin julienne strips approximately 1 1/4 inches long. Add the nori strips to the other ingredients and gently toss to combine. Serve with grilled chicken or thinly sliced rare roast beef.

soy beef fillet with pickled ginger

makes 15–20

10½ ounces beef fillet, trimmed
3 tablespoons soy sauce
3 tablespoons mirin
1 tablespoon vegetable oil
sea salt and freshly ground black pepper, to season
1 cup shredded daikon
½ cup shredded cucumber
1 teaspoon grated fresh ginger
1 teaspoon sesame oil
1 nori sheet
2 tablespoons pickled ginger

Cut the beef fillet in half lengthwise. Put 2 tablespoons each of the soy sauce and mirin in a ceramic dish. Add the beef, then cover and marinate in the refrigerator overnight, turning the beef occasionally.

Heat the oil in a frying pan over high heat. Sear the beef for several minutes on each side. Season with sea salt and freshly ground black pepper. Cover with foil and allow to cool.

Put the daikon, cucumber, fresh ginger, sesame oil, and the remaining soy sauce and mirin in a bowl and toss together. Slice the nori sheet into ¾ inch-wide strips and then cut each strip in half.

Slice the beef very thinly. Put a little of the daikon salad and a small piece of pickled ginger onto one of the beef slices and roll it up. Place it onto a strip of nori and roll again. Put the parcel onto a plate, with the loose end of the nori facing down. Repeat with the remaining ingredients. Serve at room temperature.

seared beef with arugula

makes 20

1 tablespoon freshly ground black pepper
12 ounces beef fillet, trimmed
1 tablespoon olive oil
salt, to season
20 large arugula leaves
1/3 cup pesto (see basics)

Rub freshly ground black pepper into the surface of the beef fillet. Heat the oil in a frying pan over high heat and sear the fillet for 4 minutes on each side or until browned. Remove, season with salt, and cover with foil. When cool, slice the beef into twenty very thin slices.

Put the arugula on a clean surface. Place a thin slice of beef on top of each leaf. Add a teaspoon of pesto and roll up. Serve immediately.

polenta and zucchini salad with blue cheese dressing

serves 4

- 1/2 cup polenta
- 2 teaspoons butter
- 6 zucchini, sliced diagonally
- 3 tablespoons olive oil
- 2 tablespoons crumbled blue cheese
- 4 tablespoons extra-virgin olive oil
- 1 tablespoon red wine vinegar
- 3 cups firmly packed baby spinach

Preheat the oven to 400°F. Bring 1 1/2 cups of salted water to a boil in a large saucepan. Slowly pour in the polenta and stir until the polenta thickens and begins to draw away from the side of the saucepan. Stir in the butter, then remove from the heat. Pour the polenta onto a tray or flat plate until 1/2 inch thick. Allow to cool. Put the zucchini on a baking sheet and brush with a little olive oil. Bake until soft and cooked through. Slice the cooled polenta into rectangular chips and put on a greased baking sheet. Brush the polenta with a little oil and bake for 10 minutes.

To make the blue cheese dressing, combine the blue cheese, extra-virgin olive oil, and vinegar in a small bowl. Layer the zucchini, polenta, and spinach onto four serving plates and drizzle with the dressing.

lemongrass shrimp

makes 20

20 small bamboo skewers
2 lemongrass stems, trimmed and roughly chopped
1 handful cilantro leaves
4 tablespoons ground rice
1 tablespoon shaved jaggery (or brown sugar)
2 tablespoons lime juice
20 raw jumbo shrimp, peeled and deveined, with tails intact
lime wedges, to serve

Put the bamboo skewers in a bowl of cold water to soak.

Put the lemongrass, cilantro, ground rice, jaggery, and lime juice in a food processor. Process to form a thick paste. Set aside.

Open out the shrimp along the incision left after deveining, and flatten lightly with the palm of your hand. Press 1 teaspoon of the paste along this surface, then skewer the shrimp around the paste so the paste is held in place. When ready, lightly cook the shrimp on a barbecue or in a frying pan. Cook the shrimp on each side for a few minutes, or until they are orange and the flesh is opaque. Serve with lime wedges.

caramelized fennel and apple

serves 4

1 tablespoon butter
1 small fennel bulb, thinly sliced
20 sage leaves
sea salt and white pepper, to season
2 green apples, cored and thinly sliced
3 tablespoons white wine
1 teaspoon sugar

Melt the butter in a large, heavy-based frying pan over medium heat. Add the fennel and sauté until the fennel is golden and soft. Add the sage leaves and cook for a minute. Season with sea salt and white pepper, then add the apples, white wine, and sugar. Cover and cook for 3 minutes or until the apples are just beginning to soften and caramelize. Be careful not to let them get too dark. Serve with pork chops or roast pork loin.

bean and pistachio salad

serves 4-6

3 cups green beans, trimmed
14-ounce can lima beans, drained and rinsed
1 handful mint
1/2 cup pistachios, toasted
2 mandarins, zested and juiced
3 tablespoons extra-virgin olive oil
salt and freshly ground black pepper, to season

Blanch the green beans in boiling salted water for a few minutes, or until they turn bright green. Drain and rinse under cold running water.

Put the green beans in a salad bowl along with the lima beans. Add the mint, pistachios, and mandarin zest, and toss together. Blend the mandarin juice and olive oil in a small bowl. Season with salt and freshly ground black pepper. Pour the dressing over the salad and serve.

marinated artichokes

serves 4

4 globe artichokes
3 lemons, halved
4 tablespoons olive oil
8 mint leaves, finely chopped
1 handful Italian parsley, roughly chopped
1 garlic clove, crushed
sea salt and freshly ground black pepper, to season

Bring a large saucepan of salted water to a boil. Meanwhile, prepare the artichokes.

Fill a bowl with cold water. Add the juice of one of the lemons to the water. Trim the artichoke stalks to within 3/4 inch of the artichoke head, then pull away the outer leaves until the base of the leaves look yellow and crisp. With a sharp knife, slice away the top third of the artichokes. Rub the artichoke with the cut side of the lemon. Put the artichoke in the water. Trim the remaining artichokes. Remove the artichokes from the water and scrape out the central choke and pull out any spiky inner leaves. Return to the water. When the water is boiling, add the artichokes, weigh them down with a plate, and simmer for 20 minutes. Test that the artichokes are cooked by pushing the tip of a knife into each one just above the stem—it should be tender. Drain well, then slice in half.

Put the artichokes in a large dish with the oil, herbs, garlic, and juice from the remaining lemons. Season with sea salt and freshly ground black pepper.

avocado salsa

serves 4

- 1 avocado, finely diced
- 1 Lebanese (short) cucumber, finely diced
- 1 red chili, seeded and finely diced
- 1 tablespoon finely diced red onion
- 3 tablespoons lime juice
- 1/2 teaspoon sea salt
- 1 handful cilantro leaves
- 1 tablespoon extra-virgin olive oil

Put the avocado, cucumber, chili, onion, lime juice, and sea salt in a bowl. Add the cilantro and olive oil. Lightly stir to combine.

Serve the salsa with some grilled chicken, shrimp, or white-fleshed fish. The salsa can also be served with warm tortillas or on bruschetta.

baked apples

serves 6

2 tablespoons balsamic vinegar
1 tablespoon honey
1 tablespoon butter, melted
freshly ground black pepper, to season
3 apples, quartered and cored

Preheat the oven to 350°F. Put the balsamic vinegar in a small bowl with the honey, butter, and a generous amount of freshly ground black pepper. Toss the apples in the balsamic marinade. Put the apples, skin side down, in a small baking dish and drizzle with the remaining marinade. Bake for 30 minutes, then turn the apples over and bake for 15 minutes more. Serve with roast pork.

sautéed spinach

serves 4

1 bunch spinach (1 pound)
1 tablespoon butter
sea salt and freshly ground black pepper, to season

Rinse the spinach under running water. Remove the stalks and roots and roughly chop the leaves. Heat the butter in a large saucepan over medium heat and add the chopped spinach. Cover with a lid and cook for 2 minutes. Remove from the heat. Season with sea salt and freshly ground black pepper before serving. Serve with poached eggs or grilled swordfish.

bean salads

serves 4

pistachio salad

4 cups green beans, blanched
2 tablespoons olive oil
2 tablespoons orange juice
1 teaspoon balsamic vinegar
1/4 cup pistachios, roughly chopped
sea salt and freshly ground black pepper, to season

Toss the beans with the olive oil, orange juice, balsamic vinegar, and pistachios. Season with sea salt and freshly ground black pepper.

black bean salad

4 cups green beans, blanched
2 tablespoons Chinese black beans, rinsed
1/4 cup sliced almonds, lightly toasted
1 large red chili, seeded and finely sliced
1 tablespoon lime juice
2 tablespoons olive oil
sea salt and freshly ground black pepper, to season

Toss the beans with the Chinese black beans, almonds, chili, lime juice, and olive oil. Season with sea salt and freshly ground black pepper.

minted peas

serves 4

10 mint leaves
2 1/2 cups peas
1 tablespoon olive oil
freshly ground black pepper, to season

Bring a saucepan of salted water to a boil. Add the fresh peas and mint, reserving the nicer mint leaves to fold through the finished dish. Boil the peas for 3–5 minutes, or until they are cooked through. Drain the cooked peas. Stir in the mint leaves, olive oil, and lots of freshly ground black pepper.

coconut greens

serves 4

2 cups green beans, trimmed
2 3/4 cups snap peas, trimmed
1 tablespoon olive oil
2 garlic cloves, crushed
1 tablespoon very finely chopped lemongrass, white part only
1 teaspoon paprika
1/2 cup unsweetened coconut milk
2 tablespoons fish sauce
1 teaspoon shaved jaggery (or brown sugar)

Blanch the beans and peas in boiling salted water for 2 minutes, or until they turn bright green. Drain and rinse under running cold water. Set aside.

Heat the oil in a wok or large frying pan over medium to high heat. Add the garlic, lemongrass, and paprika. Stir-fry for 1 minute, then add the coconut milk, 1/2 cup of water, the fish sauce, and the jaggery. Reduce the heat and simmer for 5 minutes, stirring to dissolve the jaggery. Add the beans and snap peas and cook for 1 minute. Spoon into a serving bowl. Serve with steamed rice and chicken or fish.

nori rolls

makes 24 slices

rice dressing

4 tablespoons rice vinegar
4 tablespoons sugar
1 tablespoon sea salt

filling ingredients

1 1/2 cups sushi rice
4 tablespoons pickled ginger
1 teaspoon wasabi
4 nori sheets
2 Lebanese (short) cucumbers, thinly sliced into long lengths
1 avocado, thinly sliced into long lengths
1 small-to-medium daikon, julienned

To make the rice dressing, put the rice vinegar in a saucepan with the sugar and sea salt. Heat over medium heat, stirring until the sugar has dissolved. Remove from the heat. Allow to cool. Cook the sushi rice, then spoon the rice onto a tray. Pour the rice dressing over the rice and allow to cool.

Put the ginger and wasabi in separate bowls. Lay a nori sheet onto a sushi mat. Put several spoonfuls of the rice onto the nori sheet. Dip your hands in water, then press out the rice until it covers three-quarters of the nori sheet, leaving one edge clear of rice. Lay some of the cucumber, avocado, daikon, and pickled ginger across the rice. Dab a little of the wasabi along the edge of the nori sheet where there is no rice. Using the sushi mat, tightly roll the nori and rice, starting from the rice-covered end. Once rolled, set aside and continue with the remaining nori sheets and ingredients. Using a sharp knife, cut each sushi roll into six rounds, about 3/4 inch wide.

chicken and pink grapefruit salad lavash with pastrami fig and goat cheese salad with a szechuan dressing artichoke, bean, and feta salad pea and lettuce soup arugula, pear, and parmesan salad warm salad of chestnuts and brussels sprouts fried haloumi zucchini and snap pea salad salmon and lime fish cakes potato salad summer salad with toasted pistachio dressing sesame chips with lime

02 light meals

shrimp green chicken salad asparagus with smoked salmon wilted spinach salad calamari with chili dressing chicken and miso soup octopus salad crab and watercress salad shrimp with cilantro and lime goat cheese salad with celery pear and parsley

spinach and ricotta omelette

serves 4-6

4 tablespoons butter
1 onion, thinly sliced
1/2 teaspoon ground cumin
pinch of freshly grated nutmeg
1 bunch spinach (about 1 pound), washed and trimmed
6 eggs, separated
4 tablespoons roughly chopped Italian parsley
2 tablespoons finely chopped dill
3/4 cup ricotta cheese
sea salt and freshly ground black pepper, to season
3 tablespoons grated fresh Parmesan cheese
whole-wheat toast, to serve

Melt 1 tablespoon of the butter in a large, heavy-based frying pan over medium heat. Add the onion, cumin, and nutmeg and cook until the onion is soft. Add the spinach, cover, and steam for 2 minutes. Remove from the heat and allow to cool. Meanwhile, beat the egg whites in a bowl until they form stiff peaks.

Squeeze the spinach of any excess liquid and roughly chop. Combine the spinach and onion mixture in a bowl with the egg yolks, parsley, dill, and ricotta. Season with sea salt and freshly ground black pepper, then lightly fold in the egg whites.

Return the frying pan to high heat and melt the remaining butter. Pour in the spinach and egg mixture, reduce the heat to medium, and cook for about 2 minutes. Sprinkle with Parmesan and place under a hot broiler until the omelette is golden. Serve with toast.

lavash with pastrami

serves 4

- 2 red bell peppers
- 1 English (long) cucumber
- 4 pieces lavash or other unleavened bread
- 8 slices pastrami
- 4 dill pickles, thinly sliced
- 1 cup firmly packed baby spinach

Put the two whole bell peppers under a hot broiler and cook until the skin is beginning to blacken and blister all over. Transfer them to a bowl and cover with plastic wrap. When the bell peppers have cooled, remove the skin and seeds and thinly slice the flesh. Set aside. Slice the cucumber into long, thin strips using a vegetable peeler.

Put one piece of lavash on a clean, dry surface. Put two pieces of pastrami along one side and top with some strips of cucumber, sliced bell pepper, dill pickles, and spinach leaves. Roll up and set aside. Repeat with the remaining three pieces of bread. Cut the lavash rolls in half and serve.

fig and goat cheese salad with a szechuan dressing

serves 4

1 teaspoon Szechuan peppercorns, crushed
1 teaspoon honey
2 teaspoons balsamic vinegar
3 tablespoons olive oil
1–2 heads butter lettuce
8 ripe figs, quartered
1 1/4 cups soft goat cheese
baguette, to serve

To make the Szechuan dressing, put the peppercorns, honey, vinegar, and oil in a small bowl and stir until the honey has dissolved. Make the salad by arranging the smallest lettuce leaves on four salad plates. Divide the figs between the plates and crumble the goat cheese over each. Drizzle with the dressing and serve with a baguette.

artichoke, bean, and feta salad

serves 4

4 globe artichokes
2 lemons, halved
4 tablespoons olive oil
8 mint leaves, finely chopped
2 1/2 cups green beans, trimmed
3/4 cup crumbled feta cheese

Bring a large saucepan of salted water to a boil. Meanwhile, prepare the artichokes. Trim the artichoke stalks to within 3/4 inch of the artichoke head, then pull away the outer leaves until the base of the leaves looks yellow and crisp. With a sharp knife, slice away the top third of the artichokes, scrape out the central choke, and pull out any spiky inner leaves. Rub the artichokes with the cut side of a lemon. When the water is boiling, add the artichokes, weigh them down with a plate, and simmer for 20 minutes. Test that the artichokes are cooked by pushing the tip of a knife into each one just above the stem—it should be tender. Drain the artichokes upside down, then slice in half. Put in a bowl with the oil, mint, and juice from the remaining lemon halves. Season.

Blanch the beans in boiling water until they turn bright green, then rinse under cold running water. Divide the artichokes between four plates, pile the beans on top, and sprinkle on the feta. Drizzle with any remaining dressing.

pea and lettuce soup

serves 4

2 tablespoons olive oil
1 leek, thinly sliced
1 garlic clove, crushed
4 cups vegetable or chicken stock (see basics)
1 head butter lettuce, stem removed, thinly sliced
1 cup fresh peas
1 teaspoon sugar
20 mint leaves
salt and pepper, to season
finely grated fresh Parmesan cheese, to serve

Put the oil, leek, and garlic in a large saucepan and sauté until the leek is soft. Add the stock, lettuce, and peas and bring to a boil. Reduce the heat and simmer for 15 minutes, or until the peas are soft, then remove the pan from the heat. Add the sugar and mint leaves. Pour the soup mixture into a blender or food processor and blend until it is smooth. Season well. Serve with grated Parmesan cheese.

arugula, pear, and parmesan salad

serves 4

1 small bunch arugula (about 7 ounces)
2 Bosc pears, thinly sliced
1½ cups shaved fresh Parmesan cheese
extra-virgin olive oil
balsamic vinegar

Put the arugula leaves in a bowl with the pears and Parmesan cheese. Drizzle with extra-virgin olive oil and balsamic vinegar and lightly toss.

warm salad of chestnuts and brussels sprouts

serves 4

12 fresh chestnuts
8 Brussels sprouts, trimmed and cut in half
4 tablespoons butter
1 tablespoon lemon juice
salt and pepper, to season
2 tablespoons roughly chopped Italian parsley

Preheat the oven to 400°F. Cut a gash in the outer shell of each chestnut. Put on a baking sheet and roast for 15–20 minutes or until the shells split. Peel the chestnuts while they are still warm and rub off their inner skins. Any particularly stubborn ones can be boiled for 2–3 minutes to loosen the skins. Cut in half if you like.

Bring a saucepan of water to a boil. Add the Brussels sprouts and cook for 5 minutes. When the sprouts are cooked, heat the butter in a frying pan over high heat until the butter begins to turn golden brown. Add the lemon juice, chestnuts, and Brussels sprouts and toss together. Season to taste. Sprinkle with the parsley and serve.

fried haloumi

serves 4

9 ounces haloumi cheese
2 Lebanese (short) cucumbers
1/2 red onion, thinly sliced
2 handfuls mint
1 tablespoon lemon juice
3/4 cup olive oil
salt and pepper, to season

Slice the haloumi lengthwise into eight thick slices. Trim the ends from the cucumbers, cut in half, and then cut lengthwise into long, thin strips. Put the cucumber in a bowl with the onion, mint, lemon juice, and 1/2 cup of the olive oil. Toss together and season with salt and pepper. Divide the salad between four plates.

Heat the remaining oil in a frying pan over high heat. Fry each of the haloumi slices on both sides. Arrange the cheese on top of each salad and serve.

zucchini and snap pea salad

serves 4

$2^3/4$ cups snap peas, trimmed
4 zucchini, trimmed and thickly sliced
6–8 radishes, trimmed and thinly sliced
1 tablespoon lemon juice
3 tablespoons walnut oil
1 teaspoon celery salt
freshly ground black pepper, to season
2 tablespoons pepitas (pumpkin seeds), toasted

Bring a saucepan of salted water to a boil. Add the snap peas and blanch until they are bright green. Remove with a slotted spoon and rinse under cold running water. Add the zucchini to the boiling water and cook for 2 minutes. Put the zucchini and snap peas in a bowl with the radishes.

To make the dressing, combine the lemon juice, walnut oil, celery salt, and some freshly ground black pepper in a small bowl. Drizzle the dressing over the salad and sprinkle the toasted pepitas over the top.

salmon and lime fish cakes

serves 4

6 Kaffir lime leaves, 2 very finely sliced and chopped
18 ounces salmon fillets, boned and skin removed
2 cups fresh bread crumbs
2 tablespoons finely chopped cilantro leaves
2 tablespoons very finely chopped lemongrass, white part only
2 large red chilies, seeded and finely chopped
1/2 cup thinly sliced scallions
2 eggs
1 teaspoon fish sauce
1 tablespoon lime juice
1/2 teaspoon ground white pepper
4 tablespoons vegetable oil
2 limes, halved, to serve
green salad, to serve

Put 1 cup of water and the 4 whole lime leaves in a frying pan over high heat. Add the salmon, then reduce the heat and simmer, covered, for 5 minutes or until cooked through. Remove the salmon from the pan and allow to cool.

Using a fork, break up the cooled salmon and combine in a bowl with the chopped lime leaves, bread crumbs, cilantro, lemongrass, chilies, scallions, eggs, fish sauce, lime juice, and white pepper. Shape the mixture into twelve patties. Heat some oil in a nonstick frying pan over medium heat. Cook the patties in batches until they are golden brown. Drain on paper towels. Add more oil to the pan as you need it. Serve with the lime halves and a salad.

potato salad

serves 4

4 large all-purpose potatoes
6 scallions, thinly sliced
4 large handfuls Italian parsley, roughly chopped
1/2 cup chopped dill
1/2 cup olive oil
1 lemon, zested and juiced
salt and freshly ground black pepper, to season

Cut the potatoes into chunks. Put in a large saucepan of salted cold water and bring to a boil over high heat. When the water has reached boiling point, cover and remove the pan from the heat. Leave the potatoes to sit for 30 minutes. (Cooking the potatoes this way ensures they won't break up or become waterlogged.)

Meanwhile, mix the scallions, parsley, dill, olive oil, and lemon zest and juice together. When the potatoes are ready, test them with the point of a sharp knife—they should be tender and cooked through. Drain and add to the herbed dressing while they are still hot. Toss to combine and season with salt and freshly ground black pepper.

summer salad with toasted pistachio dressing

serves 4

2 Lebanese (short) cucumbers, thinly sliced
1 cup bean sprouts, trimmed
1 red bell pepper, julienned
1 orange, segmented, pith removed, and thinly sliced in half lengthwise
1 bunch chives (about 3/4 ounce), chopped into 3/4-inch lengths
2 handfuls baby arugula
1 teaspoon finely grated fresh ginger
1 teaspoon honey
2 tablespoons lemon juice
1 teaspoon wasabi paste
4 tablespoons olive oil
sea salt and freshly ground black pepper, to season
1 cup pistachios, toasted and roughly chopped

Put the cucumbers, bean sprouts, bell pepper, orange, chives, and arugula in a large serving bowl. Toss to combine.

To make the pistachio dressing, put the ginger, honey, lemon juice, wasabi, and olive oil in a small bowl. Stir well to combine. Season with a little sea salt and freshly ground black pepper. Add the pistachios to the dressing, then pour the dressing over the salad.

sesame chips with lime shrimp

serves 4

1 tablespoon finely chopped lemongrass, white part only
1 red chili, seeded and finely chopped
2 tablespoons lime juice
3 tablespoons olive oil
16 large raw shrimp, peeled and deveined with tails intact
1 handful cilantro sprigs
1/3 cup lemon mayonnaise (see basics)

sesame chips

1 egg
1/2 cup sesame seeds
1 cup peanut oil
8 wonton skins

Put the lemongrass, chili, lime juice, and olive oil in a bowl. Add the shrimp to the bowl, cover, and refrigerate for several hours.

To make the sesame chips, whisk the egg and 1 tablespoon of water in a small bowl. Put the sesame seeds in another small bowl. Heat the oil in a deep frying pan or wok over high heat. Brush the egg wash onto one of the wonton skins, then sprinkle with the sesame seeds. When the oil is hot, add the wonton skin and fry for 30 seconds, or until it is puffed and golden brown. Remove from the pan and drain on a paper towel. Repeat with the remaining wonton skins.

Heat a large, nonstick frying pan over medium heat. Add the shrimp and cook for 2–3 minutes, or until they are pink and beginning to curl up.

To assemble, put a sesame chip on each serving plate. Top with the shrimp, a few cilantro sprigs, a large dollop of lemon mayonnaise, and the remaining sesame chips.

green chicken salad

serves 4

2 boneless, skinless chicken breasts, poached and shredded
3 scallions, thinly sliced diagonally
1 large handful roughly chopped mint
1 large handful roughly chopped cilantro leaves
1/4 cup dried Asian fried onions
2 tablespoons sesame seeds, toasted
2 tablespoons lime juice
2 tablespoons fish sauce
2 teaspoons grated fresh ginger
2 red chilies, seeded and finely chopped
1 tablespoon shaved jaggery (or brown sugar)

Combine the chicken, scallions, mint, cilantro, fried onions, and sesame seeds in a large bowl. In a small bowl, mix together the lime juice, fish sauce, ginger, chilies, and jaggery. Stir until the jaggery has dissolved, then pour the dressing over the chicken salad.

asparagus with smoked salmon

serves 4

1 egg yolk
1 teaspoon Dijon mustard
1 tablespoon lemon juice
1/2 teaspoon sugar
1 pinch salt
1/2 cup light olive oil
16 asparagus spears, ends trimmed
1 cup croutons
1/2 bunch watercress (about 7 ounces), stalks removed
8 slices smoked salmon
freshly ground black pepper, to season

Whisk together the egg yolk, mustard, lemon juice, sugar, and salt. Slowly add the olive oil, whisking until the mixture becomes thick and creamy. Set aside.

Bring a saucepan of water to a boil. Cook the asparagus for 4 minutes or until tender. Refresh under cold water. Drain the asparagus well. Put the dressing, asparagus, croutons, and watercress in a large bowl and toss together. Divide the salmon between four plates and top with a pile of the salad. Season with freshly ground black pepper.

wilted spinach salad

serves 4

- 2 bunches spinach (about 2 pounds), washed and trimmed, well drained
- 12 kalamata olives, pitted and roughly chopped
- 1 garlic clove, finely chopped
- 2 tablespoons finely chopped mint
- 1 small red onion, halved and thinly sliced
- 2 tablespoons red wine vinegar
- 1 1/3 cups crumbled feta cheese
- 1/2 cup olive oil
- 1 cup croutons

Roughly chop the large spinach leaves and put the chopped leaves and small whole leaves in a large heatproof bowl. Add the olives, garlic, mint, onion, and vinegar, then sprinkle with the feta cheese. Heat the olive oil in a frying pan over high heat until the oil is almost smoking, then pour it over the salad. Stand back, as some of the oil may splatter when you do this. Toss the ingredients again and pile into a serving bowl. Sprinkle with croutons and serve immediately.

calamari with chili dressing

serves 4

1 small red chili, seeded and finely chopped
4 tablespoons rice wine vinegar
2 tablespoons extra-virgin olive oil
1 teaspoon sesame oil
2 teaspoons superfine sugar
2 teaspoons fish sauce
1 tablespoon lime juice
1 tablespoon finely chopped mint
1 bunch watercress (14 ounces), stalks removed
1/3 daikon (about 5 ounces), julienned
21 ounces baby squid, cleaned

To make the chili dressing, combine the chili, vinegar, olive oil, sesame oil, sugar, fish sauce, lime juice, and mint in a bowl. Toss the watercress sprigs and the daikon together in a bowl. Pile onto four small plates.

Using a sharp knife, score the surface of the squid tubes in a crisscross pattern. Heat a nonstick frying pan over high heat. Cook the squid for 1–2 minutes or until it is just white. Remove from the heat and slice into thick, bite-size pieces. Put the squid into the bowl with the chili dressing and toss to coat. Place the squid pieces on the salad and spoon the remaining dressing over the squid.

chicken and miso soup serves 4

- 6 dried shiitake mushrooms
- 4 cups chicken stock (see basics)
- 1 1/4-inch piece fresh ginger, peeled and cut into thick rounds
- 1 small cinnamon stick
- 2 boneless, skinless chicken breasts, finely sliced diagonally
- 6 scallions, trimmed and cut into 1/4-inch lengths
- 8 baby corn, cut in half lengthwise
- 2 tablespoons white miso
- 1 1/3 cups snap peas, trimmed

Put the mushrooms in a bowl and cover with 1 cup of hot water. Allow to soak for 10 minutes. Remove the mushrooms and strain the liquid into a large saucepan. Discard the tough stems of the mushrooms and thinly slice the caps. Add them to the pan along with the stock, ginger, and cinnamon. Bring to a boil, then reduce the heat and simmer for 10 minutes. Remove the cinnamon stick. Add the chicken, scallions, and corn. Simmer for 5 minutes, then add the miso and peas. Heat the soup until nearly boiling. Ladle into four bowls.

octopus salad

serves 4

6–8 small all-purpose potatoes
1 teaspoon sea salt
2 lemons, juiced
4 garlic cloves
10–12 thyme sprigs
8 small baby octopuses, cleaned
2 handfuls baby arugula
2 handfuls Italian parsley
1/3 cup small black olives
sea salt and freshly ground black pepper, to season
3 tablespoons extra-virgin olive oil
1 lemon, cut into wedges

Put the potatoes in a large saucepan and fill with cold water. Add the sea salt, lemon juice, garlic, and thyme. Bring to a boil and cook for 10 minutes, then add the octopuses and cook for 10 minutes. Remove from the heat and allow the octopuses and potatoes to cool in the water. When they are cool, remove and cut into bite-size chunks.

Divide the arugula and most of the parsley between four plates. Arrange the potatoes and octopuses over the leaves. Scatter with the olives and garnish with the remaining parsley. Lightly season with sea salt and freshly ground black pepper. Drizzle with the olive oil and serve with lemon wedges.

marinated bocconcini salad

serves 4

3 tablespoons extra-virgin olive oil
1 handful Italian parsley
1 tablespoon thyme
10 mint leaves, roughly torn
2 tablespoons finely chopped chives
10 basil leaves, roughly torn
4 bocconcini (fresh baby mozzarella cheese), cut into quarters
sea salt and freshly ground black pepper, to season
24 small black olives
2 tablespoons balsamic vinegar

Put the olive oil, parsley, thyme, mint, chives, and basil in a bowl. Add the bocconcini and toss to coat in the herbs. Season with sea salt and freshly ground black pepper. Set aside to marinate in the refrigerator for 1 hour, or overnight.

Pile the bocconcini in a serving bowl. Scatter the olives over the cheese. Drizzle with balsamic vinegar and season to taste.

crab and watercress salad

serves 4

scant $1/2$ cup tamarind water (see basics)
2 tablespoons shaved jaggery (or brown sugar)
2 tablespoons fish sauce
2 tablespoons lime juice
$1\frac{1}{2}$ cups fresh cooked crabmeat
2 tablespoons light olive oil
2 tablespoons finely chopped cilantro leaves
sea salt and freshly ground black pepper, to season
1 bunch watercress (14 ounces), stalks removed
1 yellow bell pepper, julienned
3 large red chilies, seeded and thinly sliced
2 scallions, thinly sliced

To make the dressing, put the tamarind water, jaggery, fish sauce, and lime juice in a small bowl and stir until the jaggery has dissolved. Set aside.

Put the crabmeat in a bowl and break up the meat into fine threads. Add the olive oil and cilantro and stir until well combined. Season with sea salt and freshly ground black pepper.

Mix the watercress, bell pepper, chilies, and scallions in a large bowl. Drizzle with the dressing and toss to coat all the indgredients in the dressing. Divide the salad between four plates and top with a large spoonful of the crabmeat.

shrimp with cilantro and lime

serves 4

2 tablespoons chopped cilantro root
2 tablespoons grated fresh ginger
2 garlic cloves, roughly chopped
1 lemongrass stem, white part only, roughly chopped
1/2 cup vegetable oil
1 teaspoon ground coriander
20 large raw shrimp, peeled and deveined with tails intact
1 large handful cilantro leaves
1/4 cup lime juice
1/2 cup olive oil
1/2 teaspoon sugar
1 pinch salt
20 small bamboo skewers, soaked in hot water for 20 minutes

Put the cilantro root, ginger, garlic, lemongrass, vegetable oil, and ground coriander in a blender and blend to form a smooth paste. Put the shrimp in a ceramic or glass dish and pour the paste over the shrimp. Cover and leave to marinate in the refrigerator for at least 1 hour.

Combine the cilantro leaves, lime juice, olive oil, sugar, and salt in a bowl and set aside.

Place a shrimp on each bamboo skewer. Grill on a moderately hot barbecue for 5 minutes. Serve with a drizzle of the cilantro dressing.

goat cheese salad with celery, pear, and parsley

serves 4

1 tablespoon white wine vinegar
3 tablespoons extra-virgin olive oil
sea salt and freshly ground black pepper, to season
3 celery stalks, thinly sliced
3 Asian pears, thinly sliced
1 handful Italian parsley
1/4 cup flaked almonds, toasted
1 cup fresh goat cheese

Put the vinegar and olive oil in a large bowl. Season with sea salt and freshly ground black pepper. Stir to combine, then add the celery, pears, parsley, and almonds. Toss, then pile onto a serving platter. Crumble the goat cheese over the salad and serve.

bell pepper salad with tuna and egg

serves 4

1 garlic clove, crushed
1 1/2 tablespoons red wine vinegar
3 tablespoons olive oil
1 green bell pepper, finely diced
1 yellow bell pepper, finely diced
3 ripe tomatoes, cut into wedges
1 bunch baby arugula (about 5 ounces)
6-ounce can tuna, drained
4 hard-boiled eggs, quartered
5 handfuls Italian parsley,
roughly chopped
salt and pepper, to season

Combine the garlic, vinegar, olive oil, bell peppers, and tomatoes in a bowl. Pile four plates with the arugula and top with the bell pepper salad, tuna, boiled eggs, and parsley. Season with salt and pepper.

smoked trout fish cakes with wilted spinach

serves 4

- 2 all-purpose potatoes, peeled
- 2 scallions, thinly sliced
- 7 ounces smoked trout, boned and skin removed
- 1 bunch dill (about 2 1/2 ounces), finely chopped
- 2 tablespoons finely chopped chives
- salt and pepper, to season
- 1 egg
- 1/4 cup vegetable oil
- 2 tablespoons butter
- 1 1/2 bunches spinach (about 26 ounces), washed and trimmed
- lemon halves, to serve

Cut the potatoes into chunks. Put in a saucepan of salted cold water. Bring to a boil and cook at a simmer until tender. Drain and mash the potatoes. Add the scallions, smoked trout, dill, and chives to the mash and mix together. Season and stir in the egg. Form the mixture into sixteen patties.

Heat the oil in a frying pan and cook the patties in batches until they are golden brown and crisp on both sides. Drain on paper towels.

Heat the butter in another pan and sauté the spinach for about 1 minute, or until it is just wilted. Pile the spinach onto four plates and top with the fish cakes. Serve with the lemon halves.

chicken and papaya salad

serves 4

2 boneless roasted chicken breasts, roughly shredded
1/2 cup peanuts, roughly chopped
1 orange papaya, peeled, seeded, and sliced
1 Lebanese (short) cucumber, diced
2 tablespoons dried Asian fried onions
2 scallions, shredded
3 handfuls mint
salt and freshly ground black pepper, to season
16 betel leaves

dressing
1/2 cup tamarind water (see basics)
1 teaspoon soy sauce
2 teaspoons finely grated fresh ginger
1 tablespoon shaved jaggery (or brown sugar)
1/2 teaspoon ground cumin
1 large red chili, seeded and thinly sliced

To make the dressing, combine the tamarind water, soy sauce, ginger, jaggery, cumin, and chili in a bowl. Stir to dissolve the jaggery.

Add the chicken to the dressing and toss. Combine the remaining salad ingredients, except the betel leaves, in another bowl. Season with salt and freshly ground black pepper. Arrange the betel leaves on four plates and top with the salad, chicken, and any remaining dressing.

meadow mushrooms on puff pastry

serves 4

4 meadow mushrooms
2 tablespoons olive oil
1 garlic clove, crushed
sea salt and freshly ground black pepper, to taste
1 sheet puff pastry
4 handfuls arugula
3/4 cup shaved fresh Parmesan cheese
1 tablespoon balsamic vinegar

Preheat the oven to 350°F. Remove the stems from the mushrooms. Put the mushroom caps in a large bowl with the olive oil, garlic, and some sea salt and freshly ground black pepper. Toss to coat the mushrooms in the garlicky oil.

Cut the puff pastry into four squares and lay them on a baking sheet. Roll the edges of each pastry square over to form a raised edge, then put a mushroom into the center of each square. Bake for 20 minutes, or until the pastry is puffed and golden.

Tear the arugula into bite-size pieces, then toss with the Parmesan and vinegar. Season to taste. Pile the arugula salad on top of the mushroom tartlets. Serve while still warm.

chicken and pink grapefruit salad

serves 4

- 1 scallion, thinly sliced
- 2 tablespoons white wine vinegar
- 4 tablespoons extra-virgin olive oil
- 1/3 cup crème fraîche
- 2 cups shredded roasted chicken
- 2 pink grapefruits
- 3 handfuls mixed salad leaves (mizuna, corn salad, and baby spinach leaves)
- 8 walnuts, roughly chopped
- sea salt and freshly ground black pepper, to season

Combine the scallion, vinegar, olive oil, and crème fraîche in a bowl. If too thick, add a little warm water. Add the shredded chicken and toss.

Using a sharp knife, peel the grapefruit and remove the pith by slicing between each of the membranes.

Arrange a bed of mixed salad leaves on a serving platter. Top with the chicken, grapefruit, and walnuts, and season with sea salt and freshly ground black pepper.

octopus with thai dressing

serves 4

- 2 red chilies, seeded and finely chopped
- 1 garlic clove, crushed
- 1 tablespoon shaved jaggery (or brown sugar)
- 1 tablespoon lime juice
- 3 tablespoons fish sauce
- 1 tablespoon rice wine vinegar
- 3 tablespoons olive oil
- 2 tablespoons white wine vinegar
- 1 tablespoon finely chopped cilantro leaves
- 16 small octopuses, cleaned
- baby green leaf salad, to serve
- lime wedges, to serve

To make the Thai dressing, combine the chilies, garlic, jaggery, lime juice, fish sauce, and rice wine vinegar in a bowl. Add 3 tablespoons of water and stir until the jaggery has dissolved.

Mix the olive oil, white wine vinegar, and cilantro together in a large bowl and add the octopuses. Cover and leave to marinate in the refrigerator for a few hours, or preferably overnight.

Remove the octopuses from the marinade and grill on a hot barbecue or grill plate for a few minutes on each side until it looks charred around the edges and is cooked through. Serve the octopuses on the green leaf salad with the Thai dressing and lime wedges.

chicken and preserved lemon salad

serves 4

1 tablespoon sea salt
2 lemons, juiced
2 boneless, skinless chicken breasts
3 tablespoons olive oil
1 teaspoon ground cumin
1 tablespoon finely chopped preserved lemon
1 cup flaked almonds, toasted
2 handfuls cilantro leaves, roughly chopped
2 handfuls mint, roughly chopped
1/2 cup golden raisins

Bring a saucepan of water to a boil and add the salt, half the lemon juice, and the chicken. Bring back to a boil, cover, and remove the pan from the heat. Leave the chicken in the pan for 30 minutes. Remove the chicken from the water, drain well, and thinly slice against the grain.

Put the chicken in a large bowl and add the olive oil, cumin, preserved lemon, the remaining lemon juice, and the almond flakes. Toss together, then add the cilantro, mint, and golden raisins and toss again.

caesar salad

serves 4

1 teaspoon Dijon mustard
2 tablespoons lemon juice
3 eggs
scant 1 cup olive oil
3 tablespoons grated fresh Parmesan cheese
sea salt and freshly ground black pepper, to season
2 bacon slices, thinly sliced
3 slices sourdough bread, crusts removed, chopped
2 heads romaine lettuce
4 anchovies, finely chopped

Whisk together the mustard, lemon juice, and 1 egg. Pour in 1/2 cup of the olive oil, whisking constantly. Stir in the Parmesan and season with sea salt and freshly ground black pepper. Boil the remaining eggs for 6 minutes.

Heat the remaining olive oil in a frying pan over medium heat and fry the bacon until brown and crisp. As the bacon cooks, remove and drain on paper towels. Add the chopped bread to the oil and fry until golden brown.

Roughly chop the hearts of the lettuce heads and put on a serving platter. Shell and quarter the boiled eggs. Add the eggs, bacon, fried bread, and anchovies to the platter. Drizzle with the dressing.

white bean and herb soup

serves 4

2 tablespoons olive oil
2 onions, finely diced
2 celery stalks, thinly sliced
4 cups vegetable or chicken stock (see basics)
1 1/2 cups cooked white beans, such as cannellini
4 large handfuls Italian parsley, roughly chopped
10 basil leaves, finely chopped
1/2 cup light sour cream
10 mint leaves, finely chopped
crusty bread, to serve

Heat the oil in a large saucepan over medium heat. Add the onions and celery and sauté until the onions are soft and transparent. Stir in the stock and white beans and simmer for 30 minutes.

Just before serving, add the parsley and basil. Cook for 1 minute and then ladle the soup into four soup bowls. Add the sour cream, garnish with the chopped mint, and serve with thick slices of crusty bread.

salmon carpaccio

serves 4

1 small fennel bulb, trimmed
1/2 teaspoon sea salt
1 teaspoon finely chopped mint
1 teaspoon finely chopped dill
1 teaspoon sugar
1 lemon, juiced
11 ounces sashimi salmon, boned and skin removed
salted baby capers, rinsed and drained, to serve
extra-virgin olive oil, for drizzling

Cut the fennel bulb into paper-thin slices and finely chop the feathery fennel tops. Put the sliced fennel and fennel tops in a bowl with the sea salt, chopped herbs, sugar, and lemon juice. Toss to combine. Cover the salad and refrigerate for 1 hour.

Check that all the bones have been removed from the salmon fillet, then wrap it in plastic wrap and put it in the freezer for 30 minutes to firm up. Use a sharp knife to cut the chilled salmon into paper-thin strips.

Divide the salmon slices between four small plates. Top with the fennel salad, arranging it so the salmon slices can be seen through the fennel. Sprinkle with capers and drizzle with olive oil.

pear and walnut salad

serves 4

1 cup walnut halves
1/2 garlic clove
1 orange, zested and juiced
1 teaspoon sea salt
1/2 cup light olive oil
1 small bunch arugula (8 1/2 ounces)
2 beurre bosc pears
5 ounces fresh goat's cheese
salt and pepper, to season

Put the walnuts, garlic, orange zest, sea salt, and olive oil in a blender or food processor and blend to form a sauce. Toss the arugula in the orange juice and divide the leaves between four plates.

Core the pears, slice them thinly, and arrange the slices over the arugula. Top with the goat's cheese and pour the walnut dressing over the top. Season with salt and pepper.

green papaya salad

serves 4

3 tablespoons lime juice
3 tablespoons fish sauce
3 tablespoons sugar
2 large red chilies, seeded and finely chopped
1 tablespoon finely chopped mint
1 green papaya
2 tablespoons toasted peanuts, finely chopped
1 large handful cilantro leaves

To make the dressing, combine the lime juice, fish sauce, sugar, chilies, and mint in a bowl. Stir until the sugar has dissolved.

Peel the papaya and cut the flesh into pieces. Finely julienne or grate the papaya and add it to the dressing along with the peanuts and cilantro. Toss the salad ingredients together and serve immediately.

green bean salad with cherry tomatoes and haloumi

serves 4

- 1 tablespoon lemon juice
- 2 tablespoons extra-virgin olive oil
- sea salt and freshly ground black pepper, to season
- 1 1/2 cups green beans, trimmed
- 1 1/2 cups scarlet runner beans, trimmed
- 2 cups cherry tomatoes, cut into quarters
- 1 handful mint
- 1 handful basil
- 9 ounces haloumi cheese
- 1 tablespoon olive oil

Put the lemon juice and extra-virgin olive oil in a large bowl and season with a little sea salt and freshly ground black pepper.

Slice the green beans into halves and the runner beans into 1/2-inch lengths. Bring a saucepan of salted water to a boil. Add the beans and cook until they are bright green. Drain and toss the beans in the lemon juice and olive oil. When the beans are cool, add the tomatoes, mint, and basil.

Cut the haloumi into eight slices. Heat the olive oil in a frying pan over high heat and fry the haloumi on both sides until golden brown. Put one slice of haloumi on each serving plate. Top with the bean salad, then finish with the remaining haloumi slices.

watercress and duck salad

serves 4

1/2 cup sherry
1/2 cup orange juice
1 tablespoon soy sauce
1 teaspoon sesame oil
1 teaspoon sugar
1 teaspoon finely grated fresh ginger
1 Chinese roast duck (found in large Asian food markets)
1 1/4 cups snow peas, trimmed
7-ounce can water chestnuts, drained and sliced
1 bunch watercress (14 ounces), stalks removed

To make the dressing, put the sherry and orange juice in a small saucepan. Bring to a boil, then reduce the heat and simmer until the liquid has reduced by half. Pour the liquid into a bowl and add the soy sauce, sesame oil, sugar, and ginger.

Remove the skin from the roast duck. Cut the skin into thin strips, scraping off any fat. Lay the strips on a tray and put under a hot broiler until they crisp up. Drain on paper towels.

Remove the meat from the roast duck and tear it into strips. Add the meat to the bowl of dressing. Blanch the snow peas in boiling water and refresh under cold running water.

Toss the duck meat with the water chestnuts, watercress, snow peas, and crisp duck skin and serve.

coconut and green bean salad

serves 4

4 cups green beans, trimmed
2 green chilies, finely chopped
1 teaspoon grated fresh ginger
1/3 cup plain yogurt
1 lime, juiced
1 teaspoon sea salt
1/4 coconut, flesh freshly shaved
2 tablespoons vegetable oil
1 tablespoon brown mustard seeds
30 curry leaves

Bring a saucepan of water to a boil and cook the beans for 2–3 minutes or until they are bright green. Drain and refresh under cold running water.

Put the chilies, ginger, yogurt, lime juice, and sea salt in a bowl. Add the coconut and toss together.

Heat the oil in a small frying pan over medium heat, and add the mustard seeds and curry leaves. When the seeds begin to pop, take the pan off the heat. Add the seeds and leaves to the coconut mixture along with the green beans and toss together.

sesame salad

serves 4

4 tablespoons olive oil
1 tablespoon soy sauce
1 teaspoon sesame oil
2 tablespoons lime juice
1 teaspoon sugar
1 teaspoon finely grated fresh ginger
20 snow peas, trimmed
2 cups oyster mushrooms (about 5 ounces), quartered
5 handfuls cilantro leaves
1 red bell pepper, julienned
2 scallions, trimmed and thinly sliced
1 large red chili, seeded and finely chopped
salt and pepper, to season
3 tablespoons sesame seeds

To make the dressing, combine the olive oil, soy sauce, sesame oil, lime juice, sugar, and ginger in a bowl.

Blanch the snow peas in boiling water and refresh under cold running water. Slice the snow peas in half lengthwise and put in a bowl with the oyster mushrooms, cilantro, bell pepper, scallions, and chili. Add the dressing and toss together. Season to taste.

Heat a nonstick frying pan over high heat. Add the sesame seeds and lightly stir until they begin to brown. Sprinkle the seeds over the salad.

calamari and pine nut salad

serves 4

1 pound small squid
4 anchovy fillets, finely chopped
2 tablespoons olive oil
1 lemon, zested and juiced
2 garlic cloves, crushed
1/2 bunch arugula (about 5 1/2 ounces)
3 handfuls Italian parsley
1/2 cup shaved fresh Parmesan cheese
1/2 cup pine nuts, toasted

Combine the squid, anchovies, olive oil, lemon zest, and garlic in a bowl. Toss well to coat the squid in the marinade. Cover and marinate in the refrigerator for at least 1 hour.

Put a heavy-based frying pan over high heat. Cook the squid, searing it on both sides, for 1–2 minutes. Pour in the marinade and cook for 30 seconds. Turn off the heat and allow the squid to sit for a few minutes, then slice it into thin rings. Put the squid in a bowl along with the remaining ingredients, except the lemon juice. Toss together, then dress with the lemon juice.

salad of roasted potatoes and smoked trout

serves 4

4 large all-purpose potatoes, cut into wedges
sea salt, to season
1 lemon, zested and juiced
1/2 cup light olive oil
2 tablespoons finely chopped dill
14 ounces hot-smoked ocean trout, broken into pieces
2 cups firmly packed baby spinach
1 large handful Italian parsley, roughly chopped

Preheat the oven to 350°F. Put the potatoes in a baking dish with 1 cup of water. Season generously with sea salt and add the lemon zest and 4 tablespoons of the oil. Bake for 20 minutes, then turn the potatoes over and cook for 20 minutes more. Meanwhile, whisk the lemon juice with the remaining oil and the dill. Season to taste.

When the potatoes are golden brown, divide between four bowls. Top with the trout and spinach leaves, and sprinkle with parsley. Spoon the dill dressing over the salad before serving.

white chicken salad

serves 4

4 scallions, white part thinly sliced, green tops reserved
1 lemongrass stem, bruised
1 bunch cilantro (about 2 3/4 ounces)
1 tablespoon sea salt
2 boneless, skinless chicken breasts
2 cups jasmine rice
3 handfuls mint
1 large red chili, seeded and finely chopped
10 1/2 ounces silken firm tofu, cut into 4 thick slices
soy sauce, to serve
lime wedges, to serve

Put the green tops of the scallions into a large saucepan with the lemongrass and cilantro roots and stalks. Fill the pan with water, add the sea salt, and bring to a boil. Drop the chicken into the liquid, cover the pan, and remove from the heat. Leave the pan, covered, for 40 minutes. Lift the chicken out of the stock and check that it is cooked. Thinly slice the chicken across the grain. Reserve the stock.

Put the rice and 2 3/4 cups of the strained stock in a saucepan. Bring to a boil. Cover and cook for 25 minutes or until the liquid has been absorbed and the rice is tender.

Thinly slice half the mint leaves. Stir the sliced scallions, sliced mint, cilantro leaves, chili, and chicken into the rice. Divide between four bowls and top with a slice of tofu. Drizzle the soy sauce over the tofu and serve with a lime wedge and the whole mint leaves.

green tea noodles with lemongrass and soy

serves 4

2 lemongrass stems, white part only, finely chopped
1 tablespoon finely grated fresh ginger
3 1/2 tablespoons soy sauce
3 1/2 tablespoons sesame oil
1 1/2 tablespoons balsamic vinegar
2 tablespoons sugar
1 lemon, juiced
10 1/2 ounces dried green tea noodles (cha soba)
2 scallions, thinly sliced
1 bunch cilantro (about 2 3/4 ounces), leaves picked
1 red bell pepper, finely diced
1 yellow bell pepper, finely diced

Combine the lemongrass, ginger, soy sauce, sesame oil, balsamic vinegar, sugar, and lemon juice in a small bowl. Stir until the sugar has dissolved. Set aside.

Bring a large saucepan of water to a boil and add the noodles. Cook for 4–5 minutes or until al dente. Drain well and transfer the noodles to a large bowl. Drizzle with the dressing, lightly tossing to coat. Add the scallions, cilantro leaves, and bell peppers. Toss again before dividing among four bowls. Serve as a light meal or alongside some grilled shrimp or fish.

chicken and coconut soup

serves 4

1 teaspoon sesame oil
1 red chili, seeded and thinly sliced
2 boneless, skinless chicken breasts, thinly sliced across the grain
4 scallions, trimmed and sliced diagonally
1 red bell pepper, thinly sliced
6 cups chicken stock (see basics)
14-ounce can unsweetened coconut milk
3 tablespoons lime juice
1 tablespoon fish sauce
2 large handfuls cilantro leaves, chopped
2 cups snow pea shoots, cut into short lengths
salt and pepper, to season
lime wedges, to serve

Put the sesame oil, chili, and chicken in a wok or saucepan over medium heat. Stir-fry until the chicken is beginning to brown. Add the scallions, bell pepper, stock, coconut milk, lime juice, and fish sauce. Bring to a boil and simmer for 10 minutes.

At the last minute, stir in the cilantro and snow pea shoots. Season to taste with salt and pepper. Serve with lime wedges to squeeze over the soup.

smoked trout and cucumber salad

serves 4

2 English (long) cucumbers, peeled and seeded
1 tablespoon sea salt
1 smoked rainbow trout (9 ounces)
1 teaspoon sugar
1 tablespoon lemon juice
1 tablespoon finely chopped dill
1 bunch chives (3/4 ounce), finely chopped
1/2 cup whipping cream
1 bunch watercress (14 ounces), broken into sprigs

Thinly slice the cucumbers, sprinkle with the sea salt, and leave to drain in a colander for 30 minutes.

Take the skin off the trout and flake the flesh, making sure you remove all the small bones. Squeeze any liquid from the cucumber slices and put in a large bowl along with the smoked trout.

Combine the sugar, lemon juice, dill, chives, and cream. Pour the dressing over the cucumber and trout and toss to combine. Divide the watercress between four plates and top with the trout and cucumber salad.

warm salad of avocado and prosciutto

serves 4

1 teaspoon thyme
1/2 teaspoon soft brown sugar
1 teaspoon Dijon mustard
3 tablespoons extra-virgin olive oil
1 tablespoon balsamic vinegar
4 handfuls mesclun salad mix
2 avocados, thickly sliced
2 Lebanese (short) cucumbers, thinly sliced
2 tablespoons pine nuts, toasted
6 slices prosciutto

To make the dressing, combine the thyme, brown sugar, mustard, olive oil, and vinegar in a small bowl.

Put the mesclun on a serving plate. Arrange the avocados, cucumbers, and pine nuts on top.

Slice the prosciutto into 1 1/2-inch pieces and broil or fry until it is crisp and golden. Put the hot prosciutto into the salad dressing, toss together, then pour it over the salad.

polenta pancakes with spinach and smoked salmon

serves 4

1 cup milk
2 lemons, juiced
1 egg, lightly beaten
3/4 cup self-rising flour
1/2 cup polenta
1/2 teaspoon baking powder
1/2 teaspoon salt
2 1/2 tablespoons unsalted butter
1 tablespoon olive oil
2 handfuls baby spinach
12 slices smoked salmon
1 tablespoon salted baby capers, rinsed and drained

Combine the milk and half the lemon juice in a small bowl. Stir in the egg. Combine the flour, polenta, baking powder, and salt in a large bowl. Add the milk mixture and whisk to form a thick batter. Set aside for 30 minutes.

Meanwhile, heat the remaining lemon juice in a saucepan over medium heat and whisk in the butter. Remove from the heat when the butter has melted.

Heat a nonstick frying pan over medium heat and add the olive oil. Spoon 3 tablespoons of batter into the pan for each pancake. Cook until the underside is golden brown, then flip over and cook for another minute. Repeat with the remaining batter. Top each pancake with spinach, smoked salmon, capers, and the lemon butter.

coconut chicken salad

serves 4

2 tablespoons finely chopped lemongrass, white part only
1 teaspoon shaved jaggery (or brown sugar)
3 tablespoons lime juice
1 cup unsweetened coconut milk
1 teaspoon sesame oil
2 boneless, skinless chicken breasts
3 handfuls mint
1/4 coconut, flesh shaved and toasted
2 cups snow pea shoots
2 Lebanese (short) cucumbers, thinly sliced
2 tablespoons sesame seeds, toasted
lime wedges, to serve

Preheat the oven to 350°F. To make the dressing, put the lemongrass, jaggery, 2 tablespoons of lime juice, and the coconut milk in a small saucepan over low heat. Simmer for 10 minutes, stirring occasionally to dissolve the jaggery. Remove from the heat and allow to cool.

Put the sesame oil and the remaining lime juice in a bowl. Add the chicken, toss in the oil and juice, then transfer to a baking dish. Drizzle the chicken with the remaining marinade, cover with foil, and bake in the oven for 30 minutes. Remove the chicken and allow to cool.

Roughly shred the chicken and put it in a serving bowl. Pour on the dressing, then add the mint, coconut, shoots, and cucumber. Toss together. Sprinkle with sesame seeds and serve with a wedge of lime.

smoked tofu and sesame salad

serves 4

1/2 cup sesame seeds, toasted
1 teaspoon sugar
1 1/2 tablespoons soy sauce
1 teaspoon fresh ginger juice
1 teaspoon rice vinegar
14 ounces Chinese greens or broccolini, cut into pieces
7 ounces smoked tofu, cut into cubes
2 scallions, thinly sliced diagonally
sesame seeds, to garnish

Put the toasted sesame seeds, sugar, soy sauce, ginger juice, and vinegar in a blender with 1/3 cup of water. Blend to form a rough paste. Transfer to a small bowl.

Blanch the greens in boiling salted water for 1 minute or until they turn bright green and are tender. Pile the cooked greens on a serving platter with the tofu. Gently pour the sesame dressing over the salad. Garnish with the scallions and sesame seeds.

shrimp and lemongrass soup

serves 4

12 raw jumbo shrimp
3 lemongrass stems
$1^{1/4}$ cups oyster mushrooms (about $3^{1/2}$ ounces)
$1^{1/3}$ cups enoki mushrooms (about $3^{1/2}$ ounces)
6 Kaffir lime leaves
2 scallions, thinly sliced
$1^{1/2}$ cups bean sprouts, trimmed
3 limes, juiced
2 small red chilies
4 tablespoons fish sauce
salt and pepper, to season
cilantro and small mint leaves, to garnish

Peel and devein the shrimp, reserving the shells. Cut off the white part of the lemongrass stems, reserving the tops. Cut the lemongrass stems into 3/4-inch lengths and flatten with a cleaver or the end of a heavy-handled knife.

Heat 4 cups of water in a saucepan. Add the reserved shrimp shells and lemongrass tops. Bring the water to a boil. Strain into a large bowl, then return the stock to the pan. Add the crushed lemongrass, oyster and enoki mushrooms, and lime leaves. Return to a boil, then reduce the heat and simmer for 3–4 minutes. Add the shrimp and, as they start to turn pink, add the scallions, bean sprouts, lime juice, chilies, and fish sauce. Stir well, and season. Ladle into four warmed bowls. Garnish with cilantro and mint.

steamed chicken with cashew and mint salad seared shrimp with mint and yogurt chutney pancetta and pea risotto lamb fillets with a sesame chutney herbed chicken in paper on buttered orzo eggplant and ricotta cheese penne slow-baked tuna with lime leaves sesame beef winter chicken soup artichoke, parsley, and caper spaghetti ocean trout with salsa verde teriyaki beef with wakame salad roast chicken

03 main meals

with almond salad green pea curry pan-fried whiting thin-sliced beef with sesame roast chicken with lime pickle zucchini and caper spaghettini chili pork with snap peas braised cod spinach and watercress stir-fry duck breast with cucumber lime-marinated

steamed chicken with cashew and mint salad

serves 4

3 tablespoons lime juice
1 teaspoon sugar
2 tablespoons olive oil
1 lime, peeled with peel reserved
1 lemongrass stem, trimmed, roughly chopped
2 garlic cloves
1 tablespoon grated fresh ginger
1 large red chili, seeded and roughly chopped
1 1/2 tablespoons fish sauce
1/4 teaspoon ground white pepper
4 boneless, skinless chicken breasts
2 cups bean sprouts, trimmed
2 handfuls Vietnamese mint
1/2 cup roasted cashews, roughly chopped
steamed rice, to serve

To make the dressing, combine the lime juice, sugar, and olive oil in a bowl. Put the lime peel, lemongrass, garlic, ginger, chili, fish sauce, and white pepper in a food processor. Process to form a paste. Rub the paste over the chicken, then put in a steamer basket over a saucepan of boiling water and steam for 20 minutes.

Toss the sprouts and mint together and put on a serving platter. Slice the chicken across the grain and arrange over the salad. Scatter with cashews and drizzle with the dressing. Serve with steamed rice.

seared shrimp with mint and yogurt chutney

serves 4

16 large raw shrimp, peeled and deveined with tails intact
2 tablespoons olive oil
4 tablespoons lemon juice
1 large handful mint
1 green chili, seeded
1 teaspoon ground roasted cumin
1 teaspoon sugar
1 tablespoon grated fresh ginger
1/2 cup plain yogurt
10 snow peas, blanched
1 Lebanese (short) cucumber, diced
5 handfuls cilantro leaves
steamed white rice, to serve

Toss the shrimp in the olive oil and 1 tablespoon of the lemon juice.

Put the remaining lemon juice, mint, chili, cumin, sugar, and ginger in a blender and process to make a thin sauce. Pour the sauce into a bowl and stir in the yogurt. Season to taste.

Heat a frying pan over high heat and sear the shrimp, a few at a time, until they begin to change color and curl up. Turn over and cook for 1 minute.

Divide the snow peas, cucumber, and cilantro between four plates and top with the warm shrimp. Drizzle with the yogurt sauce and serve with rice.

pancetta and pea risotto

serves 4

2 tablespoons butter
1 onion, finely diced
8 slices pancetta, finely diced
4 sage leaves
1 cup risotto rice
4 cups hot chicken stock (see basics)
1 cup frozen peas
3/4 cup grated fresh Parmesan cheese, plus extra, to serve
1 large handful Italian parsley, roughly chopped
10 mint leaves, finely chopped
extra-virgin olive oil, for drizzling

Heat the butter in a large saucepan over medium heat. Add the onion, pancetta, and sage. Sauté until the onion is soft and transparent, then add the rice. Stir for 1 minute or until the rice is well coated and glossy.

Add 1 cup of the stock. Simmer, stirring, until it is completely absorbed. Add more stock. When the liquid has been absorbed, add the peas and more stock. Cook until all the liquid has been absorbed and then test the rice to see if it is al dente. If it needs further cooking, add a little more stock or water.

Fold in the Parmesan and work it into the risotto, then stir in the parsley and mint. Serve with a drizzle of olive oil and some more Parmesan.

lamb fillets with a sesame chutney

serves 4

- 1/4 cup sesame seeds, toasted
- 1 handful cilantro leaves
- 1 handful mint
- 3 large green chilies, seeded and finely chopped
- 3 tablespoons tamarind concentrate
- 1 tablespoon shaved jaggery (or brown sugar)
- 1 tablespoon olive oil
- 8 lamb loin fillets, trimmed (about 1 pound)
- sea salt, to season
- 3 handfuls baby arugula

To make the sesame chutney, put the sesame seeds, cilantro, mint, chilies, tamarind, and jaggery in a food processor. Add 4 tablespoons of water and process to form a smooth paste. Set aside in a small bowl.

Heat the olive oil in a large frying pan over high heat. Add the lamb fillets and sear until blood begins to show on the uncooked side. Turn over and cook for 1 minute. Remove the lamb from the pan and season with sea salt. Cover the lamb with foil and rest for 1 minute. Slice the fillets and divide between four serving plates. Serve with a spoonful of the sesame chutney and the arugula.

herbed chicken in paper on buttered orzo

serves 4

8 large sage leaves
1 leek, thinly sliced into 3-inch lengths
4 boneless, skinless chicken breasts
salt and pepper, to season
2 tablespoons butter
2 cups orzo
1 lemon, zest grated
3 handfuls Italian parsley, roughly chopped

Preheat the oven to 350°F. Lay four 8-inch squares of baking paper along the work surface. Arrange a sage leaf topped with some leek in the center of each piece of paper. Put a chicken breast on top of the leek, then season and dab with a little butter. Top with more leek and another sage leaf, then wrap up each to form small packages. Put in a baking dish and bake in the oven for 25 minutes.

Meanwhile, cook the orzo in salted boiling water until al dente. Drain and return to the warm pan along with the remaining butter, lemon zest, and parsley. Stir to combine.

To serve, pile the orzo onto four warmed plates and serve the chicken either in its wrapping or turned out. Allow the chicken juices to spill over the pasta.

eggplant and ricotta cheese penne

serves 4

- 1/2 cup vegetable oil
- 1 large eggplant, cut into 1/2-inch cubes
- 2 garlic cloves, crushed
- 1 onion, finely chopped
- 4 zucchini, thinly sliced
- 1/2 cup fresh ricotta cheese
- 20 basil leaves, torn
- 20 oregano leaves
- 1/2 cup grated fresh Parmesan cheese
- 14 ounces penne pasta
- sea salt and freshly ground black pepper, to season
- 2 tablespoons extra-virgin olive oil

Heat the oil in a frying pan over high heat. Fry the eggplant until golden and soft. Remove with a slotted spoon and drain on paper towels.

Pour off most of the oil, leaving a small amount just coating the pan. Add the garlic and onion and cook over medium heat until the onion is transparent. Add the zucchini and cook until it is just beginning to soften. Put the eggplant, zucchini, ricotta, basil, oregano, and Parmesan in a large bowl.

Meanwhile, bring a large saucepan of salted water to a boil. Add the penne and cook until al dente. Drain and add to the other ingredients in the bowl. Season with sea salt and freshly ground black pepper. Serve with a drizzle of olive oil.

slow-baked tuna with lime leaves

serves 4

21-ounce tuna fillet
sea salt, to season
15 Kaffir lime leaves
2 tablespoons pink peppercorns
1–2 cups light olive oil
lime mayonnaise (see basics), to serve
steamed potatoes and lime wedges, to serve

Preheat the oven to 235°F. Trim the tuna fillet, removing any of the dark flesh. If the fillet is particularly thick, slice it in half lengthwise. Put the tuna in a loaf pan or small casserole dish. Season with some sea salt and scatter the lime leaves and peppercorns over the tuna. Pour over enough oil to cover the fillet, and then seal the top with a lid or piece of foil. Put the tuna in the oven and bake for 45 minutes.

Lift the tuna out of the oil and serve it in thick slices with lime mayonnaise, steamed potatoes, and wedges of lime.

sesame beef

serves 4

18 ounces rump steak, thinly sliced
1 tablespoon peanut oil
1 teaspoon sesame oil
2 garlic cloves, finely chopped
3 tablespoons hoisin sauce
3 tablespoons Chinese rice wine
1 tablespoon shaved jaggery (or brown sugar)
2 tablespoons sesame seeds
8-ounce can bamboo shoots, thinly sliced
1 bunch spinach (about 1 pound), washed and thinly sliced
2 large red chilies, seeded and chopped
1 tablespoon lemon juice
rice noodles or steamed white rice, to serve

Put the steak into a bowl along with the peanut oil, sesame oil, and garlic. Stir to coat the beef well, then cover and refrigerate for a few hours.

Combine the hoisin sauce, rice wine, and jaggery in a bowl. Stir until the jaggery has dissolved, then set aside.

Add the beef mixture in batches to a hot wok and stir-fry until browned. Remove and set aside. Stir-fry the sesame seeds for 1 minute, then add the beef, bamboo shoots, spinach, and chilies. Toss for 1 minute, then add the hoisin sauce mixture. As the sauce begins to bubble, toss a few times, then add the lemon juice. Toss once more. Serve with fresh rice noodles or steamed rice.

winter chicken soup

serves 4

2 tablespoons olive oil
2 bacon slices, finely chopped
2 onions, finely diced
1 carrot, grated
1 bay leaf
2 large potatoes, diced
3 celery stalks, thinly sliced
2 boneless, skinless chicken breasts, cut into small cubes
6 cups chicken stock (see basics)
sea salt and white pepper, to season
1 handful Italian parsley, roughly chopped
1/3 cup sour cream (optional)

Put the olive oil, bacon, and onions in a large saucepan over medium heat. Sauté until the bacon is browned. Add the carrot, bay leaf, potatoes, and celery. Stir for 1 minute, then add the chicken cubes and stock. Simmer for 30 minutes. Season to taste with sea salt and white pepper. Sprinkle with parsley before serving. For a richer version, top with sour cream.

artichoke, parsley, and caper spaghetti

serves 4

12-ounce jar marinated artichoke hearts, drained and finely chopped
5 handfuls Italian parsley, roughly chopped
1 lemon, zested and juiced
2 tablespoons salted capers, rinsed well
3 handfuls baby spinach
1/2 cup grated fresh Parmesan cheese
2 tablespoons extra-virgin olive oil
14 ounces spaghetti
freshly ground pepper, to season

Bring a large saucepan of salted water to a boil.

Put the artichoke hearts, parsley, lemon zest, lemon juice, capers, spinach, Parmesan, and half the olive oil in a large bowl and stir until combined.

Cook the spaghetti in the boiling water until al dente, then drain and add to the bowl. Stir until the spaghetti is well coated, then drizzle with the remaining olive oil. Divide the pasta between four bowls, season with freshly ground black pepper, and serve immediately.

ocean trout with salsa verde

serves 4

salsa verde

1 thick slice white bread, crusts removed
4 large handfuls Italian parsley
4 anchovies
1 teaspoon salted baby capers, rinsed and drained
10 mint leaves
1 tablespoon Indian lime pickle or preserved lemon
1/3 cup light olive oil

4 ocean trout fillets (about 6 ounces each)
2 tablespoons light olive oil
boiled potatoes, to serve
sea salt, to season

To make the salsa verde, soak the bread in a bowl of water and then squeeze out any excess water—the bread should be soft but not wet. Put the bread in a food processor or blender with the parsley, anchovies, capers, mint, lime pickle, and oil. Blend to form a thick sauce.

Rinse the trout fillets in cold water and pat dry with paper towels. Heat the oil in a frying pan over high heat and add the fillets, skin side down. Press into the pan, ensuring that the heat hits the entire surface of the fillet. Cook for 2 minutes or until the skin is crisp. Turn the fish over, reduce the heat to medium, and cook for 3 minutes. Serve the trout with the salsa verde, boiled potatoes, and a sprinkling of sea salt.

teriyaki beef with wakame salad

serves 4

1 pound lean beef fillet, trimmed
3 tablespoons teriyaki sauce
1 cup dried wakame seaweed
4 tablespoons rice vinegar
3 Lebanese (short) cucumbers
1/2 teaspoon salt
2 tablespoons superfine sugar
1/2 teaspoon soy sauce
1 1/2-inch piece fresh ginger, julienned
2 red radishes, thinly sliced
1 large handful watercress sprigs
1 tablespoon black sesame seeds

Marinate the beef fillet in the teriyaki sauce for 30 minutes. Preheat the oven to 400°F. Heat a heavy-based frying pan over high heat and sear the fillet on all sides. Put in a baking dish and bake in the oven for 10 minutes. Remove and set aside.

Soak the wakame in cold water for 10 minutes or until soft. Drain, put it in a bowl, and cover with 1 tablespoon of the vinegar. Thinly slice the cucumbers diagonally and put in a separate bowl. Sprinkle with salt and set aside for several minutes. Dissolve the sugar in the soy sauce and remaining vinegar and add the ginger. Rinse the salt off the cucumber and gently squeeze dry. Combine the wakame, cucumbers, radishes, and dressing in a bowl. Toss to combine.

Thinly slice the beef. Divide it between four plates, top with the salad, and garnish with watercress and black sesame seeds.

roast chicken with almond salad

serves 4

10 saffron threads
1/2 teaspoon ground cinnamon
1 teaspoon ground ginger
2 lemons, juiced
5 tablespoons olive oil
4 chicken leg quarters
freshly ground black pepper, to season
sea salt, to season
2 green bell peppers, seeded and diced
1/2 cup flaked almonds, toasted
1 handful Italian parsley
1 tablespoon finely chopped preserved lemon
arugula, to serve

Put the saffron in a small bowl with 3 tablespoons of boiling water. Leave to steep for 2–3 minutes. Meanwhile, put the cinnamon, ginger, lemon juice, and 4 tablespoons of the olive oil in a large bowl. Stir to combine, then add the chicken, saffron water, and freshly ground black pepper. Cover and leave to marinate in the refrigerator for a few hours or overnight.

Preheat the oven to 400°F. Put the chicken in a baking dish, drizzle with the marinade, then season with sea salt. Bake for 40 minutes or until the chicken is cooked through.

Meanwhile, heat the remaining olive oil in a frying pan over medium heat. Cook the bell peppers until they begin to soften, then set aside in a bowl. Add the almonds, parsley, and preserved lemon to the bowl. Toss, then sprinkle over the chicken. Serve with arugula.

green pea curry

serves 4

2 tablespoons vegetable oil
2 teaspoons brown mustard seeds
1 teaspoon grated fresh ginger
1 large onion, thinly sliced
sea salt, to season
1 teaspoon ground turmeric
1 teaspoon ground cumin
1 red chili, seeded and finely chopped
2 large ripe tomatoes, cut into chunks
1 2/3 cups fresh peas
2 tablespoons finely chopped mint
salt and pepper, to taste
steamed white rice, to serve

Heat the oil in a deep frying pan and add the mustard seeds. When the seeds begin to pop, add the ginger, onion, and a little sea salt. Cook until the onion is soft. Stir in the turmeric, cumin, and chili. Cook for 1 minute, then add the tomatoes and 1/2 cup of water. Simmer for 2 minutes, then add the peas and mint. Cover and cook for 10–15 minutes or until the peas are tender. Season to taste and serve with steamed rice.

pan-fried whiting

serves 4

3 tablespoons lemon juice
1/2 cup light olive oil
2 tablespoons finely chopped mint
2 tablespoons finely chopped dill
1 garlic clove, crushed
8 whiting fillets (about 1 pound)
leaf salad, boiled new potatoes, and lemon wedges, to serve

Put the lemon juice, olive oil, mint, dill, and garlic in a large bowl and mix well. Rinse the whiting fillets in cold water and pat dry with paper towels. Toss the fillets in the marinade. Cover and leave to marinate in the refrigerator for a few hours.

Heat a large, nonstick frying pan over high heat. Add the fish and cook for 1–2 minutes each side, then remove from the pan. Add any remaining marinade to the pan and cook for 1 minute. Serve the whiting on a leaf salad with new potatoes, some of the pan juices, and a lemon wedge.

thin-sliced beef with sesame

serves 4

2 tablespoons hoisin sauce
2 tablespoons soy sauce
4 tablespoons sesame oil
1/4 cup sesame seeds, toasted
1 tablespoon honey
1 lime, juiced
1/2 teaspoon finely chopped chili
1 1/2 pounds roasted beef fillet
12 cherry tomatoes, cut into quarters
2 Lebanese (short) cucumbers, thinly sliced
1 small red onion, thinly sliced
3 handfuls cilantro leaves

Combine the hoisin sauce, soy sauce, sesame oil, sesame seeds, honey, lime juice, and chili in a small bowl.

Thinly slice the beef and put it in a large bowl. Add half of the sauce and the remaining salad ingredients and toss them together. Arrange the salad in piles in four bowls and drizzle with the remaining sauce.

roast chicken with lime pickle

serves 4

1 whole 4-pound free-range chicken
1 lemon, halved
1 onion, quartered
2 tablespoons butter
3 tablespoons Indian lime pickle, finely chopped
sea salt, to season
2 handfuls watercress sprigs
mashed potatoes and lime wedges, to serve

Preheat the oven to 400°F. Rinse the chicken and pat it dry with paper towels. Put the chicken in a roasting pan, breast side up, and stuff with the lemon and onion. Push the butter under the skin of the chicken breast. Rub the lime pickle over the chicken and lightly season with sea salt.

Bake for 1 1/4 hours, or until cooked through. Remove the chicken and check that it is cooked by pulling a leg away from the body—the juices that run out should be clear and not pink. Allow to rest for 15 minutes before carving and serving. Drizzle with some of the pan juices and garnish with watercress. Serve with the mashed potatoes and lime wedges.

zucchini and caper spaghettini

serves 4

3 tablespoons extra-virgin olive oil
2 garlic cloves, crushed
6 zucchini, grated
14 ounces spaghettini
1 large handful Italian parsley, roughly chopped
2 tablespoons salted baby capers, rinsed and drained
1 cup grated fresh Parmesan cheese

Bring a large saucepan of salted water to a boil.

Meanwhile, heat the oil in a deep frying pan over medium heat and add the garlic. Move the garlic around the pan with a spatula until it is lightly golden, then add the zucchini. Slowly braise the zucchini, stirring frequently, for about 15 minutes, or until it begins to dry out and catch on the base of the pan.

Add the pasta to the boiling water and cook until it is al dente, then drain and return to the saucepan. Add the parsley, capers, most of the Parmesan, and the zucchini. Toss together and divide the pasta between four bowls. Sprinkle with the remaining Parmesan.

steamed barramundi with warm greens

serves 4

1 tablespoon ground roasted cumin
1 teaspoon thyme
1/2 teaspoon ground turmeric
1 teaspoon sea salt
freshly ground black pepper, to season
4 barramundi fillets (about 7 ounces each)
3 tablespoons butter
3 zucchini, sliced diagonally
1 3/4 cups snap peas, trimmed
1 tablespoon lemon juice

Put a large saucepan of water on to boil for the steamer.

Meanwhile, put the cumin, thyme, turmeric, sea salt, and some freshly ground black pepper in a clean plastic bag. Rinse the fish fillets in cold water and pat dry with paper towels. Add the fish fillets to the bag and shake the bag to coat the fish in the spices.

Melt the butter in a large frying pan over medium heat. Add the zucchini slices and sauté until they begin to soften. Add the snap peas and lemon juice. Cover the pan and steam the peas for 2–3 minutes or until bright green.

Put the fish on a plate in a steamer basket. Place over the saucepan of simmering water and steam for about 5 minutes. Serve the fish with the lemony greens.

chili pork with snap peas

serves 4

3 tablespoons hoisin sauce
2 tablespoons Chinese rice wine
1 tablespoon finely grated fresh ginger
1/2 teaspoon red chili flakes
2 teaspoons sesame oil
1 garlic clove, crushed
14 ounces pork fillet, thinly sliced
1 tablespoon peanut oil
1 red bell pepper, thinly sliced
3 cups snap peas, trimmed
1 cup bean sprouts, trimmed
basil, to garnish
steamed rice or warm noodles, to serve

Combine the hoisin sauce, rice wine, ginger, chili flakes, sesame oil, and garlic in a large bowl. Add the sliced pork and stir to coat the pork in the marinade. Cover and refrigerate for several hours. Remove the pork from the bowl and reserve the marinade.

Heat a wok over high heat and add the peanut oil. Add the bell pepper and snap peas and stir-fry until the bell pepper is beginning to soften. Remove from the pan and set aside. Stir-fry the pork in batches until brown. Return all of the pork and vegetables to the wok along with the bean sprouts and reserved marinade. Stir-fry until the sauce begins to bubble. Garnish with basil leaves and serve with steamed rice or warm noodles.

braised cod serves 4

4 cod fillets (about 7 ounces each)
salt and white pepper, for rubbing
1 tablespoon olive oil
2 garlic cloves, thinly sliced
4 scallions, thinly sliced
2 tablespoons finely chopped dill
1 cup white wine
1 lemon, zested and juiced
1 large handful roughly chopped Italian parsley
1 tablespoon butter
steamed snow peas, to serve

Rinse the fish fillets in cold water and pat dry with paper towels. Rub the fillets with salt and white pepper.

Heat the oil in a nonstick frying pan and sauté the garlic until it is lightly golden. Add the scallions, dill, white wine, lemon zest, and lemon juice, and bring to a boil. Add the fish and cover the pan. Reduce the heat and simmer for 8 minutes. Remove the fish pieces from the cooking liquid and arrange on a warmed serving platter.

Return the pan to high heat and boil the liquid until it has reduced by half. Add the parsley and butter, swirling the pan until the butter has melted. Pour the sauce over the fish. Serve with steamed snow peas.

spinach and watercress stir-fry

serves 4

- 1 tablespoon vegetable oil
- 2 tablespoons finely chopped lemongrass, white part only
- 1 small red chili, seeded and thinly chopped
- 2 red bell peppers, thinly sliced
- 1/2 cup canned water chestnuts, roughly chopped
- 1 bunch spinach (1 pound), thinly sliced
- 1 bunch watercress (14 ounces), stems removed
- 1 tablespoon light soy sauce
- 1 teaspoon soft brown sugar
- 1 tablespoon fish sauce
- steamed jasmine rice or fresh rice noodles, to serve

Heat the oil in a wok or large frying pan over medium to high heat. Add the lemongrass and chili and cook for 1 minute. Add the bell peppers and cook for 1 minute, then add the water chestnuts, spinach, and watercress. Stir-fry for 1 minute, or until the leaves are beginning to wilt. Add the soy sauce, sugar, and fish sauce. Toss together. Serve with steamed jasmine rice or rice noodles.

duck breast with cucumber

serves 4

1/2 cup brown sugar
3 teaspoons grated fresh ginger
1 orange, zested and juiced
4 boneless duck breasts
2 teaspoons sesame oil
1 tablespoon sesame seeds
6 Lebanese (short) cucumbers, halved and sliced diagonally
1 handful garlic chives, cut into lengths
1 tablespoon soy sauce
rice, to serve

Put the brown sugar, 2 teaspoons of the ginger, and the orange zest in a bowl and mix together. With a sharp knife, make several diagonal cuts across the skin of the duck breast. Rub the sugar mixture into the surface of the skin. Marinate in the refrigerator for several hours or overnight.

Preheat the oven to 350°F. Put the duck breasts in a roasting pan and roast for 10–12 minutes. Remove the duck, cover, and keep warm.

Heat the sesame oil in a wok and add the sesame seeds and remaining ginger. As soon as the seeds begin to brown, add the cucumbers and chives. Toss for 1 minute, then add the soy sauce, orange juice, and duck juices. Put the duck under a hot broiler for 1 minute to crisp up the skin. Slice the duck and arrange on the cucumber. Serve with rice.

lime-marinated fish

serves 4

2 Kaffir lime leaves, thinly sliced
2 limes, juiced
1 red chili, seeded and finely chopped
1 teaspoon fish sauce
2 tablespoons grated fresh ginger
3 tablespoons olive oil
1 bunch cilantro (about 2 3/4 ounces)
4 cod fillets (5 1/2 ounces each)
tomato rice (see basics)

Combine the lime leaves, lime juice, chili, fish sauce, ginger, and olive oil in a large bowl. Remove the stems and roots from the cilantro and wash carefully. Finely chop them and stir into the marinade. Add the fish and toss to coat. Cover and leave to marinate in the refrigerator for 15–20 minutes.

Heat a frying pan over medium heat and add the fish fillets. Sear on one side for 3 minutes, then turn the fish over and cook for 3 minutes or until cooked through.

Put a large spoonful of the tomato rice on each of the serving plates. Garnish with some cilantro leaves and top with the fish fillets.

poached chicken with cilantro

serves 4

1/2 bunch cilantro (about 1 1/2 ounces)
3 lemons
1 tablespoon sea salt
4 boneless, skinless chicken breasts
5 large handfuls Italian parsley
1 garlic clove, roughly chopped
1/2 cup olive oil
salt and pepper, to season
2 Lebanese (short) cucumbers, cut into chunks
leaf salad, to serve

Remove the roots and stems from the cilantro and put them into a large saucepan of water. Add the juice of 1 lemon and the sea salt, and bring to a boil. When the water is boiling, add the chicken. Cover, then remove the pan from the heat. Leave covered for 1 hour.

To make the dressing, put half the cilantro leaves, the parsley, garlic, and the juice of the 2 remaining lemons into a blender or food processor. Blend everything together while slowly pouring in the oil. Season to taste.

When the chicken is cooked, drain and slice thinly across the grain. Toss the chicken with the dressing, cucumbers, and the remaining cilantro leaves. Serve with a leaf salad.

salmon fillets with a tamarind sauce

serves 4

3 tablespoons tamarind water (see basics)
1 teaspoon fish sauce
1 teaspoon sesame oil
1 teaspoon soy sauce
1 teaspoon honey
4 salmon fillets (5 ounces each), skin removed
1 tablespoon sesame seeds
steamed rice, cilantro leaves, and lime wedges, to serve

Combine the tamarind water, fish sauce, sesame oil, soy sauce, and honey in a large glass or plastic bowl. Rinse the salmon fillets in cold water and pat dry with paper towels. Add to the tamarind mixture. Cover and marinate in the refrigerator for 1 hour or overnight.

Heat a nonstick frying pan over high heat and sear the fish fillets, shaking off any excess marinade before you put them in the pan. When the fillets begin to brown, flip them over and reduce the heat. Pour the remaining marinade into the pan and sprinkle the tops of the fillets with sesame seeds. Simmer for 5–8 minutes, or until the fillets are just cooked through and the marinade has reduced to a thick sauce. Serve with rice, cilantro, and lime wedges.

barley risotto with wilted greens

serves 4

1 tablespoon butter
2 garlic cloves, crushed
1 tablespoon thyme
3 onions, thinly sliced
1 cup pearl barley
1 lemon, zest grated
4 cups chicken stock (see basics)
2/3 cup grated fresh Parmesan cheese, plus extra to serve
1 tablespoon olive oil
2 pounds kale or water spinach, roughly chopped

Melt the butter in a large saucepan over medium heat and add the garlic and thyme. Cook for a few minutes, then add the onions and cook until softened. Mix in the barley and lemon zest. Stir for a few minutes until the barley is well coated and glistening.

Add 1 cup of the stock and simmer, stirring until all the stock has been absorbed. Continue to add the stock a little at a time until it has all been absorbed by the barley. Just as the last of the stock has been absorbed, stir in the Parmesan.

Meanwhile, heat a frying pan or wok over high heat and add the oil. Toss in the kale and quickly stir-fry until just cooked. Spoon the risotto into four warmed bowls, top with the greens, and sprinkle with the extra Parmesan.

stir-fried jumbo shrimp

serves 4

3 tablespoons peanut oil
28 ounces raw jumbo shrimp, peeled and deveined with tails intact
$1^1/_4$-inch piece fresh ginger, peeled and julienned
2 red bell peppers, thinly sliced
2 yellow bell peppers, thinly sliced
2 zucchini, thinly sliced lengthwise and sliced diagonally into thin strips
4 tablespoons Chinese rice wine
2 tablespoons soy sauce
1 teaspoon sesame oil
lime wedges and garlic chives, to garnish
steamed rice, to serve

Heat a wok over medium heat and add the peanut oil. Add the shrimp and stir-fry for 1 minute. Add the ginger, bell peppers, and zucchini, and stir-fry for 1 minute. Add the rice wine and simmer for 1 minute. Pour in the soy sauce and sesame oil, toss for 1 minute, then remove from the heat. Garnish with lime wedges and garlic chives, and serve with steamed rice.

mint and kaffir chicken

serves 4

4 boneless, skinless chicken breasts
8 Kaffir lime leaves
2 tablespoons shaved jaggery (or brown sugar)
1 garlic clove
2 teaspoons fish sauce
15 mint leaves
3 tablespoons olive oil
cilantro leaves, to garnish
1 3/4 cups snap peas, trimmed, blanched, and sliced diagonally
steamed rice, to serve

Slice the chicken breasts into four pieces lengthwise and put in a bowl. Using a pair of kitchen scissors, finely cut the lime leaves, and put them in a food processor or blender with the jaggery, garlic, fish sauce, mint, and olive oil. Process for 1 minute. Pour the marinade over the chicken and stir so the chicken is well coated. Cover and marinate in the refrigerator for 1 hour or overnight.

Heat a nonstick frying pan and cook the chicken for 3–4 minutes on each side. Garnish with cilantro and serve with the snap peas and steamed rice.

steak with caramelized rosemary scallions

serves 4

1 tablespoon butter
8 scallions
4 rosemary sprigs
1 teaspoon sugar
3/4 cup red wine
1 teaspoon balsamic vinegar
1 teaspoon olive oil
4 fillet steaks (about 7 ounces each)
salt and pepper, to season
mashed potatoes, to serve

Heat the butter in a saucepan over medium heat and add the scallions. Toss until golden and beginning to soften. Add the rosemary and cook until the scallions are caramelized on the outside. Add the sugar and swirl it around the pan until it has dissolved. Pour in the red wine and balsamic vinegar. Allow the sauce to simmer for a couple of minutes to reduce the liquid by half.

Heat a heavy cast-iron frying pan over high heat and add the olive oil. When it begins to smoke, add the steaks and sear them until the uncooked surface begins to look slightly bloody. Turn the steaks over and cook for 1 minute. Season and allow the steaks to rest for a few minutes in the pan. Spoon the scallions over the steaks and serve with mashed potatoes.

whiting fillets with herb butter

serves 4

1/2 bunch watercress (7 ounces)
1 handful Italian parsley
2 tablespoons chopped chives
1 garlic clove, chopped
2 small pickled gherkins, chopped
3 anchovies
1 tablespoon salted capers, rinsed and drained
1/4 teaspoon white pepper
1/2 cup butter, softened
1 teaspoon olive oil
8 whiting fillets (about 1 pound)

Remove the top leafy sections of the watercress stalks, discarding any of the thicker stalks and wilted leaves.

Put the parsley, chives, garlic, gherkins, anchovies, capers, white pepper, and butter in a food processor or blender. Process to form a smooth paste. Lay a large piece of plastic wrap on a clean surface, and spoon the flavored butter in a line. Roll up to form a log, and refrigerate until you are ready to use it.

Heat the olive oil in a large, nonstick frying pan over high heat. Cook the whiting for 1–2 minutes on each side, then remove from the pan. Serve on a bed of the watercress topped with a few slices of the herb butter.

winter vegetable chicken

serves 2

1/4 cup all-purpose flour
2 teaspoons sea salt
1 teaspoon ground roasted cumin
2 chicken drumsticks
2 chicken thighs
1 carrot, peeled and cut into small chunks
1 turnip, peeled and cut into small chunks
1 parsnip, peeled and cut into small chunks
1 onion, sliced
2 celery stalks, trimmed and sliced
1 leek, washed and sliced
1 cup chicken stock (see basics) or water
roughly chopped Italian parsley, to serve

Preheat the oven to 350°F. Put the flour, sea salt, and cumin in a bowl and toss the chicken pieces so they are well covered with the seasoned flour.

Put half the vegetables into the base of a casserole dish and top with the chicken (shake off any excess flour). Add the remaining vegetables and stock, and cover the dish with a lid or foil. Cook for 1 hour 20 minutes. Remove from the oven, sprinkle with parsley, and serve immediately.

steamed fish with cucumber and herbs

serves 4

- 2 lemongrass stems, finely chopped
- 1/4 cup superfine sugar
- 5 tablespoons fish sauce
- 4 whitefish fillets (7 ounces each), sliced into thick strips
- 1 red chili, seeded and finely chopped
- 2 teaspoons finely grated fresh ginger
- 4 tablespoons lime juice
- 1 tablespoon shaved jaggery (or brown sugar)
- 1 large handful mint
- 1 large handful cilantro leaves
- 1 1/2 handfuls basil
- 3 Lebanese (short) cucumbers, cut into chunks

Combine the lemongrass, sugar, and 4 tablespoons of the fish sauce in a bowl. Add the fish strips and toss the fish in the mixture to coat well. Leave to marinate for 15–20 minutes.

Put the chili, ginger, lime juice, jaggery, and remaining fish sauce in a bowl. Stir until the jaggery has dissolved. Add the herbs and cucumber, and put the salad on a serving platter.

Put the fish on a plate in a bamboo or metal steamer basket and place over a saucepan of simmering water. Cover and steam for 3–4 minutes. Toss the fish gently through the salad while hot.

lemon and thyme lamb cutlets

serves 4

1 bunch lemon thyme (3/4 ounce)
12 lamb cutlets, French trimmed
3 tablespoons lemon juice
3 tablespoons olive oil
6 large fingerling or salad potatoes (about 20 ounces)
3/4 cup black olives
1 large handful Italian parsley, chopped
3 tablespoons olive oil
salt and pepper, to season
green salad, to serve

Put half the lemon thyme in a container and lay the lamb cutlets on top. Cover with the remaining thyme, lemon juice, and olive oil, making sure the cutlets are well coated in the marinade. Leave to marinate in the refrigerator for at least 1 hour or preferably overnight.

Cut the potatoes into large chunks. Put them in a large saucepan of salted cold water and bring to a boil over high heat. When the water has reached boiling point, cover the pan with a lid and remove from the heat. Leave the potatoes to sit for 30 minutes.

Take the cutlets out of the marinade and cook on a heated grill for 2–3 minutes on each side. Set aside.

Drain the potatoes and return to the saucepan along with the olives, parsley, and olive oil, stirring vigorously so the potatoes are well coated and begin to break up a little. Season to taste. Serve the cutlets with the potatoes and a green salad.

swordfish with green beans

serves 4

3 tablespoons lemon juice
1/2 cup extra virgin olive oil
1 garlic clove, crushed
1 tablespoon lemon thyme
3 cups green beans, trimmed
4 swordfish steaks (7 ounces each)
sea salt, to season
2 tablespoons light olive oil
freshly ground black pepper, to season

Combine the lemon juice, extra-virgin olive oil, garlic, and lemon thyme in a small bowl.

Bring a large saucepan of salted water to a boil. Add the beans and cook for 1–2 minutes, or until the beans are bright green and just cooked. Drain and refresh under cold running water.

Season the swordfish steaks liberally with sea salt. Put the light olive oil in a large frying pan over high heat. Add the swordfish steaks to the pan and sear for 3 minutes, or until golden brown. Turn over, reduce the heat, and cook for an additional 3–4 minutes, or until the steaks are cooked through.

Put a swordfish steak on each plate and drizzle with the lemon thyme dressing. Top the fish with some green beans and season with freshly ground black pepper.

ceviche salad

serves 4

- 1 pound whitefish fillets
- 1/2 cup lime juice
- 3 tablespoons unsweetened coconut cream
- 1 teaspoon sugar
- 1 red bell pepper, thinly sliced
- 4 scallions, thinly sliced diagonally
- 1 large red chili, seeded and finely chopped
- 2 tomatoes, seeded and diced
- 2 avocados, diced
- 4 handfuls cilantro leaves, roughly chopped

Slice the fish fillets into thin strips and put them in a glass bowl with the lime juice. Turn them over so that they are completely coated in the juice. Cover the fish and leave to marinate in the refrigerator for 2 hours. (The acidity of the lime juice partially "cooks" the fish.) Drain the fish, then toss it with the remaining ingredients. Divide the salad between four plates.

roast chicken with almond sauce

serves 4

4 whole chicken leg quarters
sea salt, for rubbing
2 tablespoons olive oil
8 lemon thyme sprigs
leaf salad, to serve

almond sauce

2 1/2 cups chicken stock (see basics)
1 cup almond meal
sea salt and white pepper, to season
1 garlic clove, crushed
2 tablespoons finely chopped Italian parsley
1/2 teaspoon sugar
1 lemon, juiced
1 pinch saffron

Preheat the oven to 400°F. Rub sea salt into the skin of the chicken, then put the chicken in a roasting pan. Drizzle the chicken with olive oil and cover with the thyme. Roast for 40 minutes, or until the chicken is cooked through. Remove from the oven and allow to rest for a minute.

To make the almond sauce, bring the stock and almond meal to a boil in a saucepan. Reduce to a simmer, season with sea salt and white pepper, and add the remaining ingredients. Simmer gently for 20 minutes. Spoon the sauce over the roast chicken and serve with a leaf salad.

seared salmon with green mango salad

serves 4

- 2 tablespoons tamarind puree
- 2 tablespoons finely grated fresh ginger
- 1 tablespoon olive oil
- 4 salmon fillets (3½ ounces each)
- 3 tablespoons lime juice
- 3 tablespoons fish sauce
- 3 tablespoons sugar
- 2 green mangoes
- 4 handfuls snow pea shoots

Combine the tamarind puree, ginger, and olive oil in a bowl. Toss the salmon in the mixture to coat well. Set aside to marinate for 30 minutes.

To make the green mango salad, combine the lime juice, fish sauce, and sugar in a bowl and stir until the sugar has dissolved. Peel the mangoes and finely julienne or grate the flesh. Add to the bowl with the dressing.

Heat a nonstick frying pan over medium heat and cook the salmon fillets for 2 minutes on each side. Serve with the mango salad and snow pea shoots.

coconut shrimp with mint and lemongrass

serves 4

2 tablespoons finely chopped lemongrass, white part only
2 tablespoons lime juice
1/2 teaspoon shaved jaggery (or brown sugar)
1 cup unsweetened coconut milk
1 tablespoon peanut oil
20 raw jumbo shrimp, peeled and deveined with tails intact
4 handfuls mint
1 cup shredded coconut, toasted
1 cup bean sprouts, trimmed
2 Lebanese (short) cucumbers, thinly sliced
1 lime, cut into wedges

Put the lemongrass, lime juice, jaggery, and coconut milk in a small saucepan over low heat. Simmer for 10 minutes, stirring occasionally to dissolve the jaggery. Remove from the heat, pour into a large bowl, and allow to cool.

Put a heavy-based frying pan over high heat and add the oil. Swirl the oil over the base of the pan, then add a few of the shrimp. Cook only as many shrimp as will comfortably fit into the pan. Sear the shrimp for a few minutes on each side, flipping them over as they change color. As the shrimp are cooked, remove and add them to the coconut sauce in the bowl. Continue until all the shrimp are cooked.

Put the mint, toasted coconut, bean sprouts, and cucumber in a bowl and toss together. Pile the salad mixture onto four plates and top with the shrimp. Drizzle with any sauce left in the bowl and serve with lime wedges.

lemongrass chicken

serves 4

1 lime, zested and juiced
1 lemongrass stem, trimmed and roughly chopped
2 garlic cloves, peeled
3/4-inch piece fresh ginger, peeled and roughly chopped
1 large red chili, seeded
1 1/2 tablespoons fish sauce
4 boneless, skinless chicken breasts
2 tablespoons olive oil
sea salt, to season
steamed white rice and Chinese greens, to serve

Preheat the oven to 400°F. Put the lime zest, lemongrass, garlic, ginger, chili, and fish sauce in a food processor or mortar and pestle and process or grind to a smooth paste. Rub the paste all over the chicken and put in a roasting pan. Drizzle with the olive oil and lime juice, and season with a little sea salt. Cover with foil and bake for 25–30 minutes. Remove from the oven and use the pointed end of a sharp knife to check that the chicken is cooked through.

Slice the chicken and serve with steamed rice, Chinese greens, and a drizzle of baking juices. You can also toss the sliced chicken with a leaf salad and sprinkle with some ground roasted peanuts.

mushroom and tofu stir-fry

serves 4

- 4 dried shiitake mushrooms
- 4 tablespoons vegetable oil
- 7 ounces firm tofu, cut into 3/4-inch cubes
- 1 teaspoon sesame oil
- 2 garlic cloves, finely chopped
- 3 scallions, finely sliced
- 1 large red chili, seeded and finely chopped
- 1 1/2 cups snow peas, trimmed
- 1 1/4 cups oyster mushrooms (about 3 1/2 ounces)
- 1 bunch watercress (14 ounces), sprigs picked
- 1 tablespoon light soy sauce
- 2 tablespoons hoisin sauce
- 1 tablespoon fish sauce
- steamed rice or fried noodles, to serve

Soak the dried shiitake mushrooms in 1/2 cup of hot water. Drain, reserving the soaking water, then remove the stalks and thinly slice the caps.

Heat 3 tablespoons of the vegetable oil in a wok. Fry the tofu over medium to high heat until golden. Remove and drain on paper towels. Wipe the wok clean. Heat the remaining vegetable oil and the sesame oil over medium heat. Add the garlic, scallions, and chili, and stir-fry for 1 minute. Add the snow peas, oyster and shiitake mushrooms, and watercress, a handful at a time, stirring constantly.

Add the soy sauce, hoisin sauce, fish sauce, and the reserved mushroom soaking water to the wok. Stir, then cover and simmer for 3 minutes. Stir in the fried tofu and gently toss all the ingredients together. Serve with steamed rice or fried noodles.

bircher granola lime madeleines drunken grapes apple and pecan crumble cake baked apples lemon and mint granita with shaved melon lime syrup puddings pear and ginger cake pear and cardamom tart apple tartlets bircher granola lime madeleines drunken grapes apple and pecan crumble cake baked apples lemon and mint granita with shaved melon lime syrup puddings pear and ginger cake pear and cardamom tart

04 sweets

apple tartlets bircher granola lime madeleines drunken grapes apple and pecan crumble cake baked apples lemon and mint granita with shaved melon lime syrup puddings pear and ginger cake pear and cardamom tart apple tartlets bircher granola lime

bircher granola

serves 4

2 cups rolled oats
1 cup apple juice
2 green apples, grated
1/2 cup plain yogurt
1/2 teaspoon ground cinnamon
fresh berries or stewed rhubarb, to serve

Put the rolled oats and apple juice in a bowl and soak for at least 1 hour or overnight. Add the grated apple to the soaked oats with the yogurt and cinnamon. Mix well and serve with fresh berries or stewed rhubarb.

lime madeleines

makes 36

2 eggs
1/4 cup superfine sugar, plus extra, to serve
1/2 teaspoon finely chopped lime zest
1 pinch salt
1/2 cup all-purpose flour
1 1/2 tablespoons unsalted butter, melted
1 teaspoon lime juice
1/2 teaspoon orange flower water

Preheat the oven to 400°F. Beat the eggs, 1/4 cup sugar, lime zest, and salt in a bowl until the mixture is pale and thick. Sift the flour over the egg mixture and lightly fold it in. Gently fold in the butter, lime juice, and orange flower water.

Grease a madeleine pan and drop a teaspoon of the batter into each of the molds. If you don't have a madeleine pan, use a shallow muffin pan. Bake in the oven for 5 minutes. Repeat with any remaining mixture. Turn out onto a wire rack to cool and sprinkle with extra sugar.

drunken grapes

serves 4

3 cups green seedless grapes (about 1 pound)
3 tablespoons brown sugar
4 tablespoons vodka
4 tablespoons crème fraîche
1/2 cup flaked almonds, toasted

Slice the grapes in half and put in a nonreactive bowl. Add the brown sugar, vodka, and crème fraîche, and stir. Cover the grapes with plastic wrap. Refrigerate for several hours.

Spoon the chilled grapes into four dessert bowls or glasses and top with the toasted almonds.

apple and pecan crumble cake

serves 10

2 cups all-purpose flour
2 teaspoons baking powder
2 cups brown sugar
2 teaspoons ground cinnamon
1/2 cup unsalted butter
1/2 cup milk
2 eggs
1 cup pecans, chopped
2 green apples, peeled and thinly sliced
whipped cream or yogurt, to serve

Preheat the oven to 350°F. Line an 8-inch springform pan with baking paper. Put the flour, baking powder, sugar, and cinnamon in a food processor, add the butter, and blend until the mixture begins to resemble bread crumbs. Put half of this mixture into the lined pan. Add the milk and eggs to the remaining mixture in the processor and blend again to make a batter, then fold in the pecans.

Arrange the apple slices over the crumble base and cover with the remaining batter. Bake for 1 hour and test with a skewer to see if the cake is cooked. Allow the cake to cool in the pan, then place on a serving plate. Serve warm with whipped cream or yogurt.

baked apples with panettone

serves 4

- 2 small loaves panettone (about 3 1/2 ounces each), or 1 large loaf
- 2 tablespoons unsalted butter
- 4 large green apples
- 1/4 cup lightly packed brown sugar
- confectioners' sugar, to serve
- cream or vanilla custard, to serve

Preheat the oven to 350°F. Line a baking dish with baking paper. Trim off the rounded top of one of the small panettone. Slice the cake into four rounds, or cut four rounds from four slices of a large panettone. Place the rounds in the dish and lightly butter.

Core the apples with an apple corer or a small sharp knife, making sure that you remove all the tough core pieces. Slice and butter the remaining small panettone, or some of the large one, then tear it into small pieces. Stuff the buttered panettone pieces into the center of the apples, alternating the pieces with a little brown sugar. Top with a teaspoon of brown sugar per apple and a pat of butter. Put the apples onto the four panettone rounds and bake for 40 minutes.

Dust with confectioners' sugar and serve with cream or vanilla custard.

lemon and mint granita with shaved melon

serves 6

1 cup superfine sugar
1 cup lemon juice
1 teaspoon orange flower water
10 mint leaves, finely chopped
1/4 each of 1 honeydew melon and 1 seedless watermelon

Put the sugar and 2 cups of water in a saucepan and heat until the sugar has dissolved. Stir in the lemon juice, orange flower water, and mint. Pour into a large plastic container and freeze for 3 hours. Remove from the freezer and break up the granita with a fork, then refreeze.

Slice the melons into very thin slices. Alternating the two types of melon, make a small stack of slices on each of six plates. Take the granita out of the freezer, break up the ice crystals by scraping with a fork, and spoon the granita over the melon.

lime syrup puddings

serves 6

4 tablespoons golden syrup or maple syrup
1 lime, zested
3 tablespoons lime juice
2 eggs, separated
1/2 cup unsalted butter
1/2 cup dark brown sugar
1 teaspoon pure vanilla extract
1 1/4 cups all-purpose flour
1 1/2 teaspoons ground ginger
1 teaspoon cream of tartar
1/2 teaspoon baking soda
1/2 cup milk
cream, to serve

Preheat the oven to 350°F. Grease six 5-fluid-ounce ramekins. Mix the golden syrup, lime zest, and lime juice together in a small bowl. Divide the mixture between the ramekins.

Beat the egg whites until stiff and then set aside. Cream the butter and brown sugar together, then add the egg yolks and vanilla. Fold in the flour, ginger, cream of tartar, and baking soda alternately with the milk. Lightly fold in the beaten egg whites. Spoon the batter into the ramekins and cover with circles of baking paper. Put the ramekins into a baking dish and fill the dish with water until it reaches halfway up the sides of the ramekins. Bake for 40 minutes, or until the puddings are cooked through. Turn the puddings out onto six plates and drizzle with cream.

pear and ginger cake

serves 8

2 tablespoons unsalted butter
1/2 cup almond meal
3 eggs
1/2 cup milk
1 3/4 cups superfine sugar
1 tablespoon grated fresh ginger
2 cups all-purpose flour
2 teaspoons baking powder
3–5 beurre bosc pears, cored and sliced lengthwise
confectioners' sugar, for dusting
whipped cream, to serve

Preheat the oven to 350°F. Grease a round 8-inch springform cake pan with half the butter. Sprinkle in half the almond meal and shake the pan to coat the base and side of the pan.

Put the eggs, milk, sugar, ginger, flour, and baking powder into a food processor or large bowl and process or mix to make a thick batter. Fold the pears into the batter and then spoon the mixture into the cake pan. Sprinkle the top of the batter with the remaining almond meal and dot with the rest of the butter.

Bake for 1 1/2 hours, check to see if the cake is cooked, then remove from the pan and cool. Dust with confectioners' sugar and serve with cream.

pear and cardamom tart serves 8

1 $3/4$ cups almond meal
$1/2$ cup unsalted butter
$2/3$ cup superfine sugar
3 eggs
$1/2$ teaspoon ground cardamom
1 tablespoon unsweetened cocoa powder
1 prebaked 10-inch short-crust pastry shell (see basics)
2 ripe beurre bosc pears

Preheat the oven to 350°F. Put the almond meal, butter, all the sugar except for 2 tablespoons, the eggs, cardamom, and cocoa powder in a food processor and blend to form a thick paste. Carefully spoon and spread the mixture into the prebaked pastry shell.

Quarter and core the pears, then slice thickly, arranging the slices in a fan over the top of the almond mixture. Bake for 20 minutes. Take the tart out of the oven and sprinkle the top with the remaining sugar. Return to the oven for 10 minutes and then test to check that the tart is cooked all the way through. Cool slightly before transferring the tart to a serving plate.

apple tartlets

makes 4

- 1/2 cup unsalted butter
- 1/2 cup sugar
- 1 teaspoon ground cinnamon
- 2 green apples, grated
- 1 teaspoon lemon juice
- 2 eggs
- 4 prebaked 4-inch pastry shells (see basics)

Preheat the oven to 350°F. Melt the butter and sugar in a saucepan. Pour the butter mixture into a bowl with the cinnamon, apple, lemon juice, and eggs. Fold together. Pour into the pastry shells and bake for 30 minutes, or until golden brown.

honeydew and pineapple whip iced lychee and mint classic daiquiri mint and ice cream smoothie mojito tropical rum blend margarita martini mint julep opal ice moroccan mint tea lychee and rum blast honeydew and pineapple whip iced lychee and mint classic daiquiri mint and ice cream smoothie mojito tropical rum blend margarita martini mint julep opal ice moroccan mint tea lychee and rum blast honeydew and

05 drinks

pineapple whip iced lychee and mint classic daiquiri mint and ice cream smoothie mojito tropical rum blend margarita martini mint julep opal ice moroccan mint tea lychee and rum blast honeydew and pineapple whip iced lychee and mint

honeydew and pineapple whip

serves 2

1 cup fresh pineapple juice
1 cup chopped honeydew melon
1 tablespoon lime juice
6 ice cubes

Put the pineapple juice, honeydew melon, lime juice, and ice cubes in a blender and blend until smooth. Pour into glasses.

iced lychee and mint

serves 2

5 canned lychees, drained, reserving 1/2 cup of the syrup
15 large mint leaves
1 tablespoon lime juice
10 ice cubes

Put the lychees, reserved syrup, mint leaves, lime juice, and ice cubes in a blender and blend until smooth. Pour into chilled glasses.

mint and ice cream smoothie

serves 2

1 cup vanilla ice cream
4 ice cubes
2 fluid ounces crème de menthe (or other mint-flavored liqueur)
6 mint leaves

Put the ice cream, ice cubes, crème de menthe, and mint leaves in a blender and blend until smooth. Pour into small, chilled glasses.

classic daiquiri

serves 1

ice
2 fluid ounces white rum
1 tablespoon lime juice
1 teaspoon triple sec
1 teaspoon superfine sugar
lime slices, to serve

Fill a cocktail shaker with ice and add the rum, lime juice, triple sec, and sugar. Shake well and strain into a chilled cocktail glass. Serve with slices of lime.

mojito

serves 1

4 mint sprigs
2 teaspoons sugar
1/2 lime, cut into quarters
2 fluid ounces white rum
4 ice cubes
soda water

Put the mint sprigs, sugar, and lime quarters in a glass and crush with a muddler or the end of a wooden spoon. Add the rum and ice cubes. Top off with soda water.

tropical rum blend

serves 2

1 fluid ounce white rum
1 fluid ounce Malibu
1 fluid ounce Midori
1 cup grapefruit juice
1 cup peeled and roughly chopped honeydew melon
ice cubes, to serve
honeydew melon wedges, to garnish

Put all the ingredients except the ice and honeydew wedges in a blender and blend until smooth. Pour into two tall glasses over the ice cubes and garnish with wedges of honeydew.

margarita

serves 1

ice
2 fluid ounces tequila
1 fluid ounce triple sec
1 tablespoon lime juice
sea salt

Fill a cocktail shaker with ice and add the tequila, triple sec, and lime juice. Shake vigorously. Wet the rim of a cocktail glass with lime juice and then dip it into sea salt. Strain the cocktail into the glass and serve.

martini

serves 1

ice
2 fluid ounces gin
1 teaspoon dry vermouth
olive or lemon peel, for garnish

Fill a cocktail shaker with ice, and add the gin. Put the vermouth into a chilled martini glass. Swirl the vermouth around the glass, then pour it out. Strain the iced gin into the glass and serve immediately with a garnish of an olive or lemon peel.

mint julep

serves 1

$1\frac{1}{2}$ teaspoons superfine sugar
10 mint leaves, plus extra, to garnish
$\frac{3}{4}$ cup crushed ice
3 fluid ounces whiskey

Put the sugar, six of the mint leaves, and a dash of water in a glass. Using a muddler or the end of a wooden spoon, mash the ingredients together until the sugar has dissolved and the mint is bruised. Fill the glass with crushed ice, and top with the whiskey. Stir well and place in the freezer for 30 minutes. Serve garnished with the remaining mint leaves.

opal ice

serves 2

$1^1/_2$ cups crushed ice, plus extra
1 fluid ounce white rum
1 fluid ounce triple sec
1 fluid ounce Midori
1 tablespoon lime juice
1 tablespoon blue curaçao

Divide the crushed ice between two large cocktail glasses. Put the rum, triple sec, Midori, and lime juice in a cocktail shaker. Add a little ice and shake well. Pour three-quarters of the mix into the glasses, then add the curaçao. Top with the remaining cocktail mix. Serve immediately.

moroccan mint tea

serves 1

4 mint sprigs
1 lemon wedge
1 star anise
1/2 cinnamon stick
1 teaspoon superfine sugar

Put the mint sprigs, lemon, star anise, cinnamon stick, and sugar in a small glass and top with boiling water. Stir well to dissolve the sugar. Drink the tea while hot.

lychee and rum blast

serves 2

- 10 canned lychees, seeded and chilled
- 1/3 cup unsweetened coconut milk, chilled
- 2 fluid ounces dark rum
- 1/4 cup lychee syrup, chilled
- 10 mint leaves

Put all the ingredients in a blender and blend until smooth. Pour into two chilled glasses and serve immediately.

pesto fresh mint sauce peanut dressing sweet ginger dressing lime and lemongrass dressing lemon and cumin dressing vinaigrette seafood marinade chicken marinade oatcakes walnut bread vegetable stock chicken stock lemon mayonnaise lime mayonnaise tomato rice mashed potatoes tamarind water short-crust pastry shell pesto fresh mint sauce peanut dressing sweet ginger dressing lime and lemongrass

06 basics

lemon and cumin dressing vinaigrette seafood marinade chicken marinade oatcakes walnut bread vegetable stock chicken stock lemon mayonnaise lime mayonnaise tomato rice mashed potatoes tamarind water short-crust pastry shell pesto fresh mint

pesto

serves 4

- 2 bunches basil, leaves picked (to give 4 1/2 ounces basil leaves)
- 1 handful Italian parsley
- 1 cup grated fresh Parmesan cheese
- 1 garlic clove
- 1/2 cup pine nuts, toasted
- 2/3 cup olive oil

Put the basil leaves, parsley, Parmesan cheese, garlic, and toasted pine nuts in a food processor, or use a mortar and pestle. Process or pound, slowly adding the oil in a steady stream until you have a spoonable consistency. Toss the pesto through freshly cooked pasta and serve.

fresh mint sauce

makes 1/2 cup

1 handful mint
2 teaspoons sugar
4 tablespoons apple cider vinegar

Put the mint on a chopping board, sprinkle with 1 teaspoon of the sugar, and finely chop. Transfer the mint to a serving bowl or pitcher and stir in the remaining sugar, the apple cider vinegar, and 2 tablespoons of boiling water. Serve with roast lamb.

peanut dressing

makes 3/4 cup

- 1 tablespoon shaved jaggery (or brown sugar)
- scant 1/2 cup tamarind water (see page 386)
- 2 tablespoons kecap manis (sweet soy sauce)
- 1 tablespoon balsamic vinegar
- 1 red chili, seeded and finely chopped
- 1 garlic clove, finely chopped
- 1/2 cup ground roasted peanuts

Combine the jaggery, tamarind water, kecap manis, and balsamic vinegar in a small bowl. Stir until the jaggery has dissolved. Add the chili, garlic, and peanuts. This dressing is delicious spooned over a salad of julienned vegetables or fresh tofu, or over thinly sliced beef with cucumber and mint.

sweet ginger dressing

makes 1 cup

1/2 cup dashi (basic Japanese soup) stock
3 tablespoons rice vinegar
4 tablespoons light soy sauce
1 tablespoon sugar
1 tablespoon finely grated fresh ginger

Put the dashi stock in a saucepan with the rice vinegar, soy sauce, and sugar. Bring to a boil, then remove from the heat and pour the hot liquid into a heatproof serving bowl. When the dressing has cooled, add the ginger. This dressing is ideal for pouring over julienned vegetable salads or mixed salads that feature crab, shrimp, or other light seafood, as well as poached chicken.

lime and lemongrass dressing

makes 1/2 cup

4 tablespoons lime juice
4 tablespoons fish sauce
2 tablespoons sugar
2 tablespoons finely chopped lemongrass, white part only
1 garlic clove, very finely chopped
2 small red chilies, seeded and finely chopped

Put the lime juice, fish sauce, and sugar in a bowl. Stir until the sugar has dissolved. Add the lemongrass, garlic, and chilies and stir to combine. This dressing is wonderful with seafood salads and simple salads of sliced cucumber, sprouts, and fresh herbs. It can also be drizzled over chilled wedges of iceberg lettuce or poured over a rice noodle salad.

lemon and cumin dressing

makes 1/2 cup

2 tablespoons lemon juice
1/2 cup olive oil
2 garlic cloves, very finely chopped
1 teaspoon ground cumin
large pinch of paprika

Combine the lemon juice, olive oil, garlic, cumin, and paprika in a bowl and stir to blend. This dressing is used on many Middle Eastern–style salads. Pour it over a salad of tomatoes and cucumbers or over lentils.

vinaigrette

makes $^{1}/_{3}$ cup

1 tablespoon lemon juice
3 tablespoons extra-virgin olive oil
sea salt and freshly ground black pepper, to season
1 garlic clove
1 teaspoon finely chopped herbs such as tarragon, oregano, basil, chervil, or thyme (optional)

Put the lemon juice and olive oil in a bowl and season with sea salt and freshly ground black pepper.

Bruise the garlic clove once with the wide blade of a large knife or a mallet. Add the garlic to the bowl, lightly stir, and allow to sit for 30 minutes to infuse. Remove the garlic and stir the dressing again. Add the herbs to the dressing, if desired. Pour over salads that feature chicken or seafood.

seafood marinade

makes 1/2 cup

1 teaspoon finely grated fresh ginger
2 tablespoons cilantro leaves
2 tablespoons lime juice
3 tablespoons olive oil

Put the ginger, cilantro, lime juice, and olive oil in a bowl and stir to combine. Add fish pieces and toss in the marinade to coat well. Allow the fish to marinate in the refrigerator for 30 minutes before cooking.

chicken marinade

makes 1/2 cup

3 tablespoons lemon juice
3 tablespoons olive oil
1 tablespoon Dijon mustard
1 teaspoon finely chopped garlic
1 teaspoon thyme
1/2 teaspoon ground white pepper
sea salt, to season

Combine the lemon juice, olive oil, mustard, garlic, thyme, and white pepper in a large bowl. Add chicken pieces and toss to coat them in the mixture. Marinate in the refrigerator for 2–3 hours. Remove the chicken from the marinade and barbecue or roast them until cooked. Season with sea salt and serve.

oatcakes

makes 24

1/2 teaspoon salt
2 cups fine oatmeal, plus extra, for rolling
1/2 teaspoon baking soda
1 1/2 tablespoons butter, melted

Preheat the oven to 315°F. In a bowl, mix the salt, oatmeal, and baking soda. Add the melted butter and 5 fluid ounces of hot water. Stir well to form a soft dough. Knead gently for 1 minute. Divide the dough into 4 portions. Roll out 1 portion thinly between two sheets of baking paper. Using a 1 1/4- to 1 1/2-inch cookie cutter, cut the dough into small rounds. Repeat with the remaining portions of dough. Put the rounds on a lined baking sheet. Bake for 15 minutes, or until pale and dry. Cool on a wire rack.

walnut bread

makes 50 slices

1 teaspoon dry yeast granules
1 teaspoon sugar
1 1/2 cups all-purpose flour
1/4 cup finely chopped walnuts
1/4 teaspoon salt
1 tablespoon walnut oil

Mix the yeast, sugar and 1/2 cup of warm water in a bowl. Cover and leave in a warm place for 10 minutes or until frothy.

Put the flour, walnuts, and salt in a bowl. Make a well in the center and add the yeast mixture. Mix to form a dough, gather into a ball, then turn out onto a floured surface and knead until smooth. Transfer to a large bowl brushed with walnut oil. Cover and leave in a warm place for 1 hour or until doubled in size. Punch down, halve the dough, and shape each portion into a sausage shape, 9 inches long and 1 1/4 inches thick. Twist each sausage to form a loose spiral and place on a greased baking sheet. Cover and leave in a warm place for 40 minutes or until doubled in size.

Meanwhile, preheat the oven to 350°F. Bake for 25 minutes or until golden and hollow-sounding when tapped. Cool, then slice each loaf into 1/4-inch slices, cutting diagonally. Reduce the oven to 315°F. Place the slices on a baking sheet and return to the oven for 8 minutes or until crisp. Allow to cool.

vegetable stock

makes about 8 cups

2 tablespoons unsalted butter
2 garlic cloves, crushed
2 onions, roughly chopped
4 leeks, roughly chopped
3 carrots, roughly chopped
3 celery stalks, thickly sliced
1 fennel bulb, trimmed, roughly chopped
1 handful Italian parsley
2 thyme sprigs
2 black peppercorns

Put the butter, garlic, and onions in a large, heavy-based saucepan over medium heat. Stir until the onion is soft and transparent. Add the leeks, carrots, celery, fennel, parsley, thyme, and peppercorns. Add 16 cups of water and bring to a boil. Reduce the heat and simmer for 2 hours. Allow to cool. Strain into another saucepan, using the back of a large spoon to press the liquid from the vegetables. Bring the stock to a boil, then reduce the heat to a rolling boil until the stock is reduced by half. If you are not using the stock immediately, cover and refrigerate or freeze it.

chicken stock

makes about 8 cups

1 whole fresh chicken
1 onion, sliced
2 celery stalks, sliced
1 leek, roughly chopped
1 bay leaf
a few Italian parsley stalks
6 peppercorns

Fill a large, heavy-based saucepan with 12 cups of cold water. Cut the chicken into several large pieces and put them in the pan. Bring just to a boil, then reduce the heat to a simmer. Skim any fat from the surface, then add the onion, celery, leek, bay leaf, parsley stalks, and peppercorns. Maintain the heat at a low simmer for 2 hours. Strain the stock into a bowl and allow to cool.

Using a large spoon, remove any fat that has risen to the surface. If a more concentrated flavor is required, return the stock to a saucepan and simmer over low heat. If you are not using the stock immediately, cover and refrigerate or freeze it.

lemon mayonnaise

makes 1 cup

2 egg yolks
1 lemon, zested and juiced
1 cup vegetable oil
sea salt, to season

Whisk the egg yolks and lemon zest and juice in a large bowl. Slowly drizzle in the oil, whisking continuously, until the mixture thickens. Continue whisking until the mixture becomes thick and creamy. Season with sea salt. If the mixture is too thick, add a little cold water to achieve the right consistency.

lime mayonnaise

makes 1 cup

2 egg yolks
1 lime, zested and juiced
1 cup vegetable oil
sea salt, to thicken

Whisk the egg yolks and lime zest and juice in a large bowl. Slowly drizzle in the oil, whisking continuously, until the mixture thickens. Continue whisking until the mixture becomes thick and creamy. Season with sea salt. If the mixture is too thick, add a little cold water to achieve the right consistency.

tomato rice

serves 4

1 tablespoon sesame oil
1 onion, finely diced
1 garlic clove, crushed
3 ripe tomatoes, diced
1 cup basmati rice
1/2 teaspoon sea salt

Put the sesame oil in a large saucepan over medium heat. Add the onion and garlic, and cook until the onion is soft and transparent. Add the tomatoes, rice, and sea salt, and stir for 1 minute, then add 1 1/2 cups of water. Increase the heat and bring the rice to a boil. Cover the pan and reduce the heat to low. Leave covered for 20 minutes and then remove from the heat.

mashed potatoes

serves 4

4 large floury potatoes, peeled
2 tablespoons milk
2 tablespoons butter
sea salt and freshly ground black pepper, to season

Cut the potatoes into pieces and cook them in simmering water for 15 minutes or until soft. Drain well. Put the potatoes back in the pan with the milk and butter. Mash them until they are smooth. Season with sea salt and freshly ground black pepper.

tamarind water

makes 2 cups

1/2 cup tamarind pulp

Put the tamarind pulp in a bowl and cover with 2 cups of boiling water. Allow it to steep for 1 hour, stirring occasionally to break up the fibers, then strain.

short-crust pastry shell

makes one 10-inch shell or four 4-inch shells

1 2/3 cups all-purpose flour
7 tablespoons unsalted butter
1 tablespoon superfine sugar
1 pinch salt

Put the flour, butter, sugar, and salt in a food processor. Process for 1 minute, then add 2 tablespoons of chilled water and pulse until the mixture just comes together. Wrap the dough in plastic wrap and chill for 30 minutes.

Roll the pastry out as thinly as possible. The easiest way to do this is to roll it out between two layers of plastic wrap. Line a greased 10-inch tart pan with the pastry and chill for 30 minutes. If making smaller tart shells then cut away rounds of pastry that are slightly larger than the required tart tin and then press the pastry into the base and sides. Prick the base, line it with crumpled baking paper, and fill with rice or baking weights. Place the pan in a preheated 350°F oven for 10–15 minutes, or until the pastry looks cooked and dry. Remove and allow to cool.

Note: Unbaked tart shells that are not used immediately can be stored in the freezer for several weeks. Put the tart shell in a preheated oven directly from the freezer (there is no need to thaw the shell first).

glossary

balsamic vinegar
Balsamic vinegar is a dark, fragrant, sweetish, aged vinegar made from grape juice. The production of authentic balsamic vinegar is controlled. Bottles of the real thing have "Aceto Balsamico Tradizionale de Modena" written on the label.

basil
The most commonly used basil is the sweet or Genoa variety, which is much favored in Italian cooking. Thai or holy basil is used in Thai and Southeast Asian dishes. To get the most out of basil leaves, they should always be torn, not chopped.

betel leaves
These are the aromatic, lacy-edged green leaves from the betel pepper. They can be found in Indian food stores.

black sesame seeds
Mainly used in Asian cooking, black sesame seeds add color, crunch, and a distinct nuttiness to whatever dish they garnish. They can be found in most Asian food stores.

bocconcini
These are small balls of mozzarella cheese, often sold sitting in their own whey. When fresh they are soft and springy to the touch and taste distinctly milky. They are available from most delicatessens.

capers
Capers are preserved in brine or salt. Salted capers have a firmer texture. Rinse off the brine or salt before using them.

Chinese black beans
These salted black beans are sold vacuum-packed or in cans in Asian food stores.

Chinese rice wine
This rice wine is similar to a fine sherry and is made from glutinous rice. It is often used in braised dishes and sauces.

choy sum
Also known as flowering Chinese cabbage. It has midgreen leaves and tender stems.

coconut cream
Slightly thicker than coconut milk, coconut cream (unsweetened) is available in cans. If unavailable, use the thick cream off the top of a can of (unsweetened) coconut milk instead.

crème fraîche
A naturally soured cream that is lighter than sour cream. It is available from delicatessens and some large supermarkets.

daikon
Daikon, or mooli, is a large white radish. Its flavor varies from mild to quite spicy. It can be freshly grated or slow-cooked in broths, and is available from most large supermarkets.

dried Asian fried onions

Crisp-fried onions are available from most Asian food stores and are sold packaged in plastic tubs or bags. They are often used as a flavor enhancer, scattered over rice and savory dishes.

feta cheese

Feta is a white cheese made from sheep or goat milk. The fresh cheese is salted and cut into blocks before being matured in its own whey. It must be kept in the whey or in oil during storage. Feta is sold in delicatessens and most supermarkets.

fish sauce

This is a highly flavored, salty liquid made from fermented fish and widely used in South Asian cuisine to give a salty, savory flavor. Buy a small bottle and keep it in the refrigerator.

ginger juice

Ginger juice is produced by finely grating fresh ginger and then squeezing the liquid from the grated flesh.

haloumi cheese

Haloumi is a semifirm sheep-milk cheese. It has a rubbery texture, which becomes soft and chewy when the cheese is cooked. Haloumi is available from delicatessens and most large supermarkets.

Indian lime pickle

Lime pickle is available from Indian food stores or large supermarkets. It is usually served as a side dish in Indian cooking.

jaggery

Light brown, unrefined sugar that comes from certain palm trees and sugar cane. It is normally sold in solid lumps which need to be grated or shaved.

Kaffir lime leaves

Also known as the makrut lime, the glossy leaves of this Southeast Asian tree impart a wonderful citrusy aroma.

lemongrass

These long, fragrant stems are very popular in Thai cuisine. The tough outer layers should be stripped off first, then the inner part can be used either finely chopped or whole in soups. Store lemongrass for up to two weeks.

mesclun

Mesclun is a green salad mix originating in Provence, France. This salad often contains a selection of young, small leaves.

mint

Mint comes in many varieties, including peppermint, spearmint, and apple mint, but the common garden variety is wonderful in salads or as a garnish.

mirin
Mirin is a rice wine used in Japanese cooking. It adds sweetness to many sauces and dressings, and it is used for marinating and glazing dishes like teriyaki. It is available from Asian food stores and large supermarkets.

mizuna
These tender young salad leaves have a pleasant, peppery flavor.

mozzarella cheese
Fresh mozzarella can be found in most delicatessens and is easily identified by its smooth, white appearance and ball-like shape.

nori
Nori is an edible seaweed sold in paper-thin sheets. To enhance the flavor, lightly toast the shiny side of the sheets over a low flame or in a low oven. Available from most large supermarkets and Asian food stores.

orange flower water
This perfumed distillation of bitter-orange blossoms is mostly used as a flavoring in baked goods and drinks.

orzo
Orzo is a small, rice-shaped pasta. It is ideal for use in soups or salads.

oyster sauce
Made from oysters, brine, and soy sauce, this thick brown sauce is a popular seasoning in Asian cuisine.

pancetta
Pancetta is salted belly of pork. It is sold in good delicatessens, especially Italian ones, and some supermarkets. Pancetta is available either rolled and finely sliced or in large pieces ready to be diced or roughly cut.

panettone
An aromatic Italian yeast bread made with raisins and candied peel, panettone is traditionally eaten at Christmas, when it is found in Italian delicatessens or large supermarkets.

papaya
This large tropical fruit can be orange, red, or yellow. It contains an enzyme that will prevent gelatin from setting, so avoid using it in gelatin recipes. Sometimes they are called pawpaws, but they are really part of the custard apple family.

pesto
Available ready-made in most supermarkets, pesto is a pureed sauce traditionally made from basil, garlic, Parmesan cheese, pine nuts, and olive oil.

pickled ginger
Japanese pickled ginger is available from most large supermarkets. The thin slivers of young ginger root are pickled in sweet vinegar and turn a distinctive salmon-pink

color in the process. The vinegar adds a sweet, gingery bite.

pink peppercorns

These are not true peppercorns but rather are the aromatic dried red berries from the tree *Schinus molle*. They have an aromatic, peppery flavor.

preserved lemon

These are whole lemons preserved in salt or brine for about 30 days, which turns their rind soft and pliable. Just the rind is used—the pulp should be scraped out and thrown away. Preserved lemon is an ingredient commonly found in Moroccan cooking. It is available from delicatessens.

prosciutto

Prosciutto is lightly salted, air-dried ham. It is most commonly bought in paper-thin slices and is available from delicatessens and large supermarkets. Both Parma ham and San Daniele are types of prosciutto.

rice paper

These edible sheets are available from most large supermarkets or specialty cookware stores. The thin sheets are most commonly used to wrap nougat and panforte.

rice paper wrappers

Rice paper wrappers are predominantly used in the cuisines of Vietnam and Thailand. They are made of rice and water paste and come in thin, round, or square sheets, which soften when soaked in water. Use to wrap around food. They are available from most large supermarkets or from specialty Asian stores.

rice wine vinegar

Made from fermented rice, this vinegar comes in clear, red, and black versions. If no color is specified in a recipe, use clear vinegar. The clear rice wine vinegar is sweeter and milder than its European counterparts or the sharper-flavored Chinese black vinegar.

risotto rice

There are three well-known varieties of risotto rice that are widely available: arborio, a large plump grain that makes a stickier risotto; vialone nano, a shorter grain that gives a loose consistency but keeps more of a bite in the middle; and carnaroli, which makes a risotto with a firm consistency.

saffron threads

Saffron should be bought in small quantities and used sparingly—not only due to the cost but also because it has a very strong flavor. Beware of inexpensive brands when buying saffron, as cheap, real saffron does not exist.

sashimi salmon

Salmon sold for making sushi and sashimi, which is intended to be eaten raw, is usually the freshest fish at the fish market. Buy a thick piece cut from the center rather than a narrower tail end.

sesame oil
Sesame oil is available in two varieties. The darker, more pungent type is made with roasted sesame seeds and comes from China, while a paler, nonroasted variety is Middle Eastern in origin.

shiitake mushrooms
These Asian mushrooms have white gills and a brown cap. Meaty in texture, they keep their shape very well when cooked. Dried shiitake are often sold as dried Chinese mushrooms.

Szechuan pepper
Made from the dried red berries of the prickly ash tree, the flavor is spicy-hot and leaves a numbing aftertaste, which can linger. Dry-fry and crush the berries for the best flavor.

tofu
This white curd is made from soybeans. Bland in taste, it takes on the flavor of the other ingredients. Usually sold in blocks, there are several different types of tofu—soft (silken), firm, sheets, and deep-fried. Refrigerate fresh tofu covered in water for up to five days, changing the water daily.

Vietnamese mint
Vietnamese mint is actually not a true mint. Also known as hot mint or laksa mint, its spicy flavor is usually found paired with spring rolls and laksas.

wakame
Wakame is a seaweed, most commonly sold in its dried form. It must be soaked in warm water until it softens and is often used in salads and soups.

wasabi
Mostly sold in tubes or in a powdered dried form (mixed to a paste with a little water), wasabi has a very hot flavor. Used to flavor sushi, sashimi, and some sauces.

water chestnuts
The edible tuber of a water plant, the water chestnut is white and crunchy and adds a delicate texture to many Southeast Asian dishes. Fresh water chestnuts can be bought from Asian food stores, but they are commonly available whole or sliced in cans.

wonton wrappers
These paper-thin sheets of dough are available either fresh or frozen from Asian food stores. They may be wrapped around fillings and steamed, deep-fried, or used in broths. The wrappers come shaped both as squares and circles.

index